The Coloured Girl in the Ring: A Guyanese Woman Remembers

by

Brenda Chester DoHarris

Tantaria Press
Lanham, MD

The Coloured Girl in the Ring:
A Guyanese Woman
Remembers

ISBN No.   0-9659444-0-9
Library of Congress No.   97-090924
1997

... if you see me
looking at your hands
listening when you speak
marching in your ranks
you must know
I do not sleep to dream, but dream to change
the world.

Guyanese poet, Martin Carter
from "Looking at Your Hands" in the 1951
collection of his poetry, *The Hill of Fire Glows Red*

For my mother,
Rebecca,
and my grandmothers,
Adelaide and Emily

Dedicated to Guyanese working people at home and abroad, and to the memories of the Guyanese martyr, Walter Rodney, and his fallen comrades, Edward Dublin and Ohene Koama

Acknowledgements

I wish to thank the Bowie State University Foundation for awarding me a grant that facilitated the publication of this book. In this regard, I extend my sincere appreciation particularly to Bowie State University President, Dr. Nathanael Pollard, Mr. Alvin Major, Dr. Avis Pointer and Dr. Joan Langdon for their interest and generous support.

Writing this work was the first leg in a journey to self, a trip eased by the following fellow travellers to whom I am greatly indebted:

my mother, Rebecca, who first taught me to write and nurtured my dreams and devotion to the Guyanese culture and my father, Clement, who first taught me to read and to love the written word;

my good friend, Gordon Matthews, for his encouragement, support and sterling example of courage, strength, patience, grace and good humour in adverse circumstances;

Gordon Vaughn-Cooke for his untiring and selfless commitment to some technological aspects of the book's production;

Glen Clarke who started work on the book's technical production and died before its completion; and his widow, Yvonne, for her continued support;

J.C. Washington for his proof-reading and editing skills;

Errol Arthur, David Hinds, David Mahesh, Maurice St. Pierre and Maxford Wolfe, friends who shared with me their insight into Indian- and African-Guyanese culture;

Carmen Subryan for her contribution to the cover, Dawn Affiliated Services, Inc. for the cover design, and Ron Ceasar for the cover photo;

my colleagues and friends, June Bobb, Yvonne Carter, Theresa Gilliams, Mary Harris, Heather Isaac, Riaz Sahibzada, Carol Thomas, Denys Vaughn-Cooke, Keith Warner, and my in-laws, Donna Alleyne-Chester and Stanley Corbin, all of whom read the manuscript and gave unsparingly of their comments and suggestions;

and last, but in no way least, Guyanese who generously and eagerly shared with me their memories of our rich cultural past and who, whenever we met, impatiently said, *"Is when dis book gun done, gyurl?"*

Coloured Girl in the Ring
(Guyanese Children's Ring Play Folk Song)

There's a coloured girl in the ring
Tra la la la la
There's a coloured girl in the ring
Tra la la la la la la
There's a coloured girl in the ring
Tra la la la la
For she like sugar and I like plum

Oh hug an' kiss yuh partner
Tra la la la la
Oh hug an' kiss yuh partner
Tra la la la la la la
Oh leh me see yuh motion
Tra la la la la la la

Oh skip across de ocean
Tra la la la la
Oh skip across de ocean
Tra la la la la la la
Oh skip across de ocean
For she like sugar an' I like plum

CHAPTER 1

I woke that morning with a faintly perceptible buzzing in my head, my eyes searching the gray gloom for the first streaks of sunlight that would signal the day. Far away in the distance in the little British Guianese village of Kitty, a cock crowed and a dog's savage bark was followed by a metallic clanging and rhythmic scraping. I knew it was Balgobin, the East Indian milkman, approaching our house on Lamaha Street. I knew too that soon I would hear his loud curses as he tried desperately to shake Rufus the Rice-eater from his trouser leg. I lay in bed knowing I was visualizing the scene quite accurately: The milkman would be performing a frantic balancing act on the rusty old *Raleigh* bike, trying to keep from falling and spilling the precious cow's milk from the enormous metal containers hanging from his handlebars by wire-like handles. He would kick out at the mangy dog, turning the handlebars sharply from side to side and causing the bike to swerve from one side of the deserted road to the other, waking the sleeping street with the loud clatter of metal. In his frustration, the milkman added loud curses to his efforts, and his cries seemed to give voice to the silent, protesting fears of Kitty's slumbering poor. But Rufus the Rice-eater was (no pun intended) dogged. He would keep his fangs hooked in Balgobin's tattered trouser hem until he developed enough speed to outstrip him. By this time, Rufus would be joined by his unruly dog pals, all barking to signal their complicity, but also showing their fear of the force of the old discarded policeman's boot that Balgobin wore.

We children called them rice-eaters—all the scrawny, stray mongrels that competed for neighbourhood rice scraps. Since we could acquire the locally grown rice cheaply, it could easily be discarded. However, few could afford to throw away the less affordable meat (when it could be secured), and often our parents instructed us to chew our bones well in an effort to get us to derive as much nutrient as we could from the meat, scarce in many Kitty households at that time.

It was 1958 and I had just become twelve. I awoke with the expectation that that day would bring me the news that I had long awaited with gut-churningly mixed anticipation. There were a limited number of scholarships available to the major government boys' and girls' high schools, and I hoped that I would be awarded one of them. For the past year, I had endured Mr. Isaac Davis' scholarship class at the local elementary school. My mother had drummed into me the importance of getting the scholarship, dangling before me the ominous prospect of a working future as a shopgirl at Booker's, the British-owned department store, or worse, should I fail to bring home the prize. As the date of the scholarship examination approached, I had watched with a growing sense of envy as friends of my own age such as my neighbours, the Braithwaites, considered "less promising" by Mr. Davis, played *catcher*, cricket and *Coloured Girl in the Ring* in the dusty schoolyard or skipped rope at the end of a day of regular classes, while we, the children of promise, tried to ignore their gleeful shrieks, laughter and play.

When he said, "less promising," Mr. Davis stressed the "s" sounds in a hissing relish that conveyed his pure contempt for anyone whom he did not consider "seriously scholarly," as he put it with sibilant menace. He felt that his first responsibility was not as much to us, wretched little ingrates who, under his watchful eye, struggled and fidgeted with the complexities of fractions, decimals and the rudiments of the Davidson and Alcock grammar book, but to our parents who paid him extra fees out of their meager, hard earned wages so that with education, we might be saved from the seeming futility of their own lives. Whenever he caught some miscreant whose eye had wandered off longingly to the school yard, he was unsparing in his use of the flexible "wild cane," administering it casually, but forcefully across the back of the boy or girl who forgot the gravity of the great enterprise upon which we had embarked.

Mr. Davis was about forty-five. He was rumoured to have been married once, but no one knew exactly how the relationship had terminated. I had often tried to imagine him locked in an amorous embrace with some physically well endowed woman, built along the lines of those I had read about in the "penny dreadful novels" (my father's description) that I sometimes consumed by flashlight under the covers after my parents had retired for the night. But his sternness was so repelling that I could never attach the warmth of gentle intimacy to him. None of us children was quite sure where he lived, and no one seemed to know anyone who knew him closely outside the immediate school environment. Since he did not make any real effort to get to know us scholarship children, our relationship with him was largely mediated by his wild cane that he called "Little Nell." Some child had started the rumour that he lived near the city jail on Camp Street, and this information, whether true or not, had only added lustre to his image in our eyes as a kind of colonial Mr. Bumble in a tropical workhouse. He was a short, dark-brown-shoe-polish-coloured man who stood very erect, and, in spite of the enervating heat, always dressed in a serge suit, crisp white cotton shirt and tie. His slightly balding, rather long head was always tilted up and backward, and his little Hitler moustache, which he sometimes stroked almost affectionately when in thought, was always neatly trimmed. He occasionally adjusted his glasses that sometimes slid slowly down his nose, and he would survey his victims, eyebrows raised, the corners of his mouth drooping, his lower lip extended. Whenever he needed to punish a serious offender, he would remove his jacket and place it carefully on the back of his chair, sometimes taking care to flick a bit of lint off it with his thumb and middle finger. He would then tuck his thumbs under his suspenders, run them up and down the length of the elastic, rock back a bit on his heels and reach for "Little Nell."

My first serious encounter with Mr. Davis and "Little Nell" came when, one day as a new student in the scholarship class, I was aware that it was my turn to work out fraction problems on the blackboard. In my fear of the cane, all my inclination towards mathematical logic fled me. I stood there before the blackboard hearing Mr. Davis demanding my reduction to their lowest terms of twenty-five over sixty—and I could not think. It seemed to me that his presence and my mental vision of the cane took up so large a space in my awareness that I could not work out a problem that had been child's play for me at my mother's kitchen table only a short time before.

"What goes into twenty-five and sixty, gyurl?" he asked, playfully smacking his serge trouser leg with the cane. Sometimes, he conveniently did not use our names so that we became an anonymous, powerless mass of "gyurl-boy."

Again, slowly and distinctly, in the manner of a court prosecutor's tired patience with a reluctant witness, he asked, "What goes into twenty-five and sixty?"

I felt the moistness of my fingers on the chalk, the awful taste of dryness in my mouth, the sudden tightness of the plaits on my head, a creeping constriction in my stomach and the back of my neck, and the awful, stifling heat of the classroom. I felt rather than heard the whine of the cane slashing through the air before it landed on my back, inflicting its searing, flame-like pain. Before I had time to recover, Mr. Davis struck again, and this time the cane connected with the back of my ear. The stinging tears flooded in my eyes.

"I ask you what goes into twenty-five and sixty and yuh stan' dere like a kunumunu?" he raged, slowly raising the cane again.

A hush had fallen over the classroom as other students, relieved at being themselves spectators—and not the spectacle on this occasion—put down their pens to enjoy the affair. It was the first time that I had ever been struck in school or beaten publicly. A combined rush of rage and humiliation coursed through me, washing over my fear. Then I felt the wetness down the insides of my legs, the sogginess of my feet in my shoes. Mr. Davis slowly lowered the cane, gingerly edging away from the pale yellow little puddle that was slowly forming around my feet.

"Go to the toilet!" he spluttered. "How *dare* you do dat here?"

The other students gradually realized what he was talking about, and their laughter rose in a slow crescendo, the boys in the back benches standing to get a better look at my soaked shoes. I walked from the classroom, small yellow bubbles popping softly up from my shoes, my wet footprints forming a track behind me, my ear and back aflame.

"Gomes!" Mr. Davis thundered, turning his slightly bulging eyes on a diminutive Portuguese boy who was now trying to cringe his way into insignificance in a back bench of the class.

The boys always tended to sit on the back benches because they felt that any mischief they executed would then go undetected. Gomes was now uncomfortably aware that just before Mr. Davis called him, he had been engrossed in deciding whether the schoolboy batsman in the yard would hit a six with the next ball bowled in a cricket game that had reached fever pitch.   Hearing his name, Gomes spun his head around suddenly and now shuddered in apprehension of what was to come.

"YYYesssir?"

"Yuh plan to spen' de res' uh yuh life helpin' yuh fadduh pickle pork in 'e salt goods shop? Pay attention!"

In disciplinary matters, Mr. Davis always abandoned his usually scrupulous use of Standard English and lapsed into Creolese. He seemed to feel that the Guianese dialect was appropriate for such circumstances.

We heard the swift buzz of the cane as Mr. Davis brought it down rhythmically on Gomes' back, stressing particular syllables with each application of the rod:

"No WONder de BRITish mekkin' suh much FUSS to gi' we we indePENdence! We less PROMisin' dan ALL de odda COLonies. We need some DISscipline!"

Gomes screamed and squirmed as though he had been bitten by a swarm of bees.

"Now get up hey an' siddung in front wid de gyurls!"

For many boys in the class, being made to sit with the girls was worse than a caning. As Gomes made his way up front, red-faced, still writhing in pain, a wave of titters passed over the class like the first droplets of a tropical drizzle on a hot dusty road.

Thirty years later in Georgetown, our nation's capital, I would encounter Manuel Gomes, now a Jesuit priest and one of the outspoken leaders of the political opposition movement for democracy. We had not seen each other since childhood. On Regent Street, in the city's warm, moist, pulsating heart, with the noises of the hawkers, traders and traffic blaring around us, we found a curious peace. We did not mention the pain and humiliation inflicted upon us by Mr. Davis, now resting quietly in the Le Repentir cemetery with the spirits of his fathers. We ignored his terrible desecration of our childhood's sanctuary, and pretending that he had left no scars on our lives, we marveled instead at our successful, if hazardous, passage into adulthood.

CHAPTER 2

A cock crowed in the distance, and his cry was taken up by his confederates who made it impossible for Kitty's denizens to sleep past sunrise. Often these cocks seemed quite close to us, almost in our very homes because the houses in Kitty are built so that they are open to the balmy breezes that blow across the seawall, originally built by the early Dutch colonizers to keep the northern low-lying coastal plain from being flooded by the muddy, often turbulent, Atlantic. Sometimes the wall was breached at high tide, and then many of our yards would be inches deep in water. After this, particularly in the rainy season, we would be cursed with a plague of mosquitoes that kept us slapping ourselves all night and swearing at their constant whining.

Many residents, including my mother, had fowl pens under their houses, ensuring a ready weekly supply of eggs or meat on special occasions like Christmas or birthdays. At the approach of a festive occasion, my mother would select a fowl which she had been fattening specially for that purpose.

"A t'ink A will take de *Senseh* dis year," she would announce to no one in particular.

"Come chi, chi, chi," she would coax the hen gently, using the special voice she reserved for my brother and me when we were ill.

She would circle the Senseh hen carefully, holding the large, specially sharpened knife. The Braithwaite children, three boys and two girls who lived in a crumbling house across from us on Lamaha Street, would take up their positions on our back steps along with my brother, Bernard, and me, an eager group of barefoot spectators, waiting to witness the execution.

The Senseh, as if sensing that her days were numbered, would be particularly elusive, her smooth feathers slipping from my mother's grasp, her cackling rising to an almost human shrillness, her feet moving so fast she seemed to be flying low in a cloud of loose feathers. We children would scream with excitement over the chase. Finally, my mother would secure her hold on the hen, and in a quick, easy motion, she would wring its neck. The dying body would continue to flutter, and my mother would then secure the Senseh's head and, sawing hard through the bone, cut it off. This part of the operation particularly delighted the little boys who had gathered on our back steps, and they were even more thrilled by the sight of the still quivering, sometimes jerking, headless body. We girls would avert our faces and grimace as my mother turned the body upside down over a metal bucket for the blood to drain off. Seeing how disturbed this made us girls, my mother would pick up the head and playfully come after us with it. We would run shrieking, our laughter blending with hers as she became a child again and momentarily forgot her struggle to keep our small family afloat.

Ours was a small cottage (built on stilts to safeguard us from flooding as were most of the other houses on Lamaha Street) with two tiny bedrooms, one in which my mother and father slept, and the other, the size of a large closet that Bernard and I occupied. My parents had done their best to furnish the little house on their small salaries: She was a nurse in the employ of the government, and he a government dispenser of medicines. In relation to what their salaries could purchase at that time, their salaries were small.

However, compared with many of our neighbors, we were somewhat better off.

The Braithwaites always seemed to be near destitution. When my mother baked bread in the "wood oven" that Grammudduh, my paternal grandmother, had built under our house, she would send over a loaf for Mrs. Braithwaite. At Christmas, she would also make sure that the Braithwaite children got apples and grapes and other such delicacies, specially imported into our country for the holidays and which many Guianese came to feel were indispensable at Christmas time. Our tiny living room contained a chiffonier ("shuvoneer" in local parlance), a reclining easy chair called a Berbice chair, a set of two Morris chairs, a couch that had belonged to my paternal grandmother and a rocking chair, one of their first pieces of furniture after my parents had set up house when they got married and in which my mother had rocked my brother and me to sleep as infants. Apart from their bed and dressing table, my parents' bedroom contained a washstand with a large basin in which rested a large jug. I was required to make sure that the basin was always clean and that the jug was always kept full of clean water from the standpipe in our yard. I also had to ensure that the large clay goblet in the kitchen remained full of drinking water, which stayed cool even in the hot dry season.

My mother was particularly proud of her chiffonier, and we could be sure of being severely dealt with if we were caught scratching its surface or setting a wet glass on it. Through its glass front, one could see the English looking tea set that had been a wedding gift to my parents and the glasses that were only used for special guests. The beaded glass decanter was removed from its place in the chiffonier at Christmastime or on other special occasions, and wine for company was poured from it into little snap glasses that were also usually kept in the chiffonier.

Just before Christmas, Bernard, a year younger than I, had to sandpaper and varnish the chiffonier and other items of furniture. Upon reflection, it seems to me now that the chiffonier had always seemed the physical embodiment of my mother's spiritual essence. Its sandpapering and varnishing and the careful removal and cleaning of its contents that she required every year appeared partly to satisfy her need for self-renewal and to re-endorse the clear certainty of her membership in a deeply convivial community.

Some years earlier, on Saturdays when my parents had left for work, I would invite over the two Braithwaite sisters who were about my age. Very carefully, we would remove parts of the tea set or the snap glasses from the chiffonier and take them down under the house where we would pretend that we were adults visiting each other and enjoying tea or snap glasses of wine. We would light a small fire under the house, using pieces of wood we had found around the yard and boil water in old discarded Carnation evaporated milk cans. Of course, it was important to restore the items to the chiffonier before my mother came home from work, or all hell would break loose. Once, I broke one of the snap glasses during one of the Braithwaite sisters' "social visits," but Gwendolyn Braithwaite quickly replaced it with a similar one from *her* mother's "shuvoneer" collection.

"Go ahead an' tek it," she had said, shoving it into my grubby hands with her own, equally as soiled.

"Ma wun mine. In fac', shi wun even know," Gwendolyn said matter-of-factly.

I could not imagine a situation in which my mother did not know the details of her chiffonier's contents. Mrs. Braithwaite, a dressmaker by trade, displayed the symptoms of a neurological illness that impaired her ability to work and at times even to walk. There were many on Lamaha Street who whispered with oracular certainty that "somebody *do* she," implying that some malevolent person was using *obeah* against Mrs. Braithwaite. At the peak of her health, she had had at least four female teenage apprentices who, while learning to hem-stitch, cut out and sew, had been simultaneously helping her with the large volume of orders for clothes. Many residents of Lamaha Street remembered when she had even had to get two sewing machines in order to cope with the work.

Her husband, Sydney, a guttersmith and general handyman, was initially never out of work. However, he soon took to drink, and while formerly his step had faltered and his speech was slightly slurred only on a Friday evening after he had been paid, he now came lurching unsteadily around the corner into Lamaha Street in the middle of the day at mid-week, so drunk he could not even ride his bicycle on which he balanced long pieces of metal needed for his work. It seemed now that he always reeked of rum, and his bicycle was frequently seen leaning against the rum shop wall near the main village square, the pieces of guttering which he used in his work lying discarded and forgotten on the road near the bicycle wheels. His children roamed the village unsupervised and ragged, and they often called Bernard and me out to play after dark, a situation my mother would not countenance. Eventually, she took it upon herself to order the Braithwaite children into their home when it got dark. They were as scared as we were of my mother's wrath, but her work did not allow her to be as vigilant of their welfare as she wished.

The Lamaha Street *spit press* reported that Mr. Braithwaite was about to lose his cottage. The more he drank, the more severe Mrs. Braithwaite's symptoms became, and the worse they became, the more he drank. My father regarded with great contempt what he saw as Mr. Braithwaite's irresponsible behavior. Sometimes Mr. Braithwaite would enter our yard, softly trying to cajole my father into coming over and having a drink with him. My father would always refuse, curtly turning away, sometimes to the business of burning garbage in our yard, tending to his small kitchen garden or retrieving the scorched Carnation milk cans from our play.

"Why yuh t'ink yuh betta dan any uh we?" Mr. Braithwaite would sneer drunkenly, his mood turning suddenly menacing.

"Who de *rass* yuh t'ink yuh is? I would have yuh know dat I play before de King at Wembley!" he would yell, seeming to wage a small war with his wobbling bicycle as he struggled to keep it upright and, at the same time, maintain his grip on his guttering materials.

The broken, yellowed teeth in his skeletal, gleaming *Nugget*'s brown face moved slightly as he spoke; his bloodshot eyes were narrowed and dead-looking as the faint odor of *Lighthouse* nicotine lingered around him. Mr. Braithwaite's trip to England as a saxophonist in a musical contingent of local Guianese was a source of great personal pride.

Increasingly, it seemed that as his life disintegrated, he conjured up the memory of the Wembley appearance to prop up his pride, a struggle as great as that he then waged with the bicycle and paraphernalia of his trade. After his little performance at the gate, with my father pretending to be engrossed in his yard work but watching him out of the corner of his eye, Mr. Braithwaite would leave for his cottage across the street where Mrs. Braithwaite sat staring vacantly from the window, slowly being stripped of her hope, her life, and the little snap glasses in her chiffonier.

CHAPTER 3

"Yuh not out uh bed yet?" My mother's voice startled me as she put her head around the door of the bedroom.

"Remember dat yuh have to tell Miss Edna dat A want two dollars black puddin' today. Tell 'er to sen' a proper length and not dat lil piece uh stupi'ness dat shi try to run pas' me hey las' week. An' tell 'er A want *souse to'*, an' she better not bring that stringy business again!"

Miss Edna had been our black pudding lady since I was two years old and could only say, "ba pud'n." She made the black pudding, a popular Guianese delicacy, by combining rice seasoned with a local herb called "married man pork" and cow's blood, and then stuffing this mixture into the cleaned intestines of the cow. The fatty souse was made from pig's cheeks or cow's face. Black pudding and souse were also popular appetizing *cuttas* at parties, and most families had their "Black Pudding Ladies" who supplied them with these and other delicacies on Saturday afternoons.

My mother's voice often took on a tougher tone when she dealt with, or referred to, the people with whom she did business, those like Miss Edna and Bahadur our grocer in the Kitty market. My mother proceeded from the assumption that these people were out to "rob her bline" and "put her in de porehouse." The only person of this kind with whom she had a more genial relationship was Agatha, our dressmaker, whom we all called 'Gatha.

"Okay Mama," I said, scrambling out of bed. I was going to be very careful not to get her in a bad mood because I did not want to fuel her irritation if the scholarship results were published that day and it turned out that I had failed.

Of course, I had no intention of relaying my mother's message to Miss Edna, whom I liked immensely. She affectionately called me "ba pud'n" and would always give me a piece of black pudding to eat when I got to her house. On Saturday mornings, her little cottage was filled with all kinds of mouth-watering smells as she, two female relatives near her own age, and a teenage girl prepared food in her hot kitchen while two kerosene stoves warmed the already steaming room, and the smell of married man pork filled one's nostrils. Here, Miss Edna's six-foot bulk would dominate the sagging little kitchen as she presided over the making of black pudding, souse, patties, *pulourie, channa,* cheese rolls, and *pine tarts.* In the afternoon, Miss Edna's females assistants would take all of these around in large baskets to the homes of various customers. Indeed, a Saturday afternoon on Lamaha Street without Miss Edna's black pudding was not to be endured.

Miss Edna wore a cotton print dress covered with a starched once-white apron now spattered with blood. The underflesh of her massive arms shook as she rinsed and scrubbed the cow's intestines, and a perspiration stain spread under her armpit and down between her breasts. Her hair was usually plaited in a tight corn row which seemed to pull her eyebrows up into her sweating brow in a look of continuous surprise. When she moved about the kitchen, her large hips and buttocks quivered under the cheap cotton print. My mother said that she well remembered the time "when Edna was *Edna*" and she had set the village men's hearts aquiver. She now wore rather sturdy, mannish, laced, black shoes, and to my unending puzzlement, considering the steaming kitchen—socks—during this Saturday operation. Her kitchen always gave me a feeling of great security; it was like the narcotic that drowned out thoughts of the scholarship exam, canings at school or my parents' struggles to provide.

Then there was the intriguing female chatter—grown-up conversations about seemingly endless problems with men... children... other women... men... My mother would have been appalled if she had known then that I was privy to such exchanges, but they gave me a glimpse of that woman's world on the edge of which I hovered curiously as over a deep, dangerous, but intensely hypnotic ravine. When I tried to eavesdrop on my mother's and 'Gatha's conversations, my mother would pointedly remind me that I had homework to do or dishes to wash. Here at Miss Edna, though, there was none of this, and I could be as relaxed as I wanted, listening and learning.

"Gyurl, yuh hear de latess wid Shirley?"

This was from Miss Edna's cousin, Miss Ada, who had come down to Kitty from the Corentyne to live with Miss Edna when Ada's *child-father* of many years had been crushed by a tractor on the rice field where he was a handy-man. Shirley, Ada's twenty-year old daughter, was working in the Blue Lantern, a bar in the seamy Tiger Bay area of the city, waitressing and doing a private striptease act there five days a week. Shirley had taken up with a married Assistant Secretary in the Civil Service, and she was showing all the signs of early pregnancy.

"Nah man. Wha' hapnin?" Miss Edna asked, her fingers maroon with cow's blood as she stuffed the intestines with the black pudding mixture.

Miss Ada was mixing the pastry for the pine tart, and her fingers were sticky with the dough. She was, like Miss Edna, in her late forties, but grayer, not as sturdy looking, with a way of pursing her lips and nervously wetting them occasionally with the tip of her tongue. Miss Edna had taken her in along with her three children, Shirley, the eldest, and two younger boys, ten years before when their father had died. She had become Miss Edna's assistant and also took in washing and ironing to supplement her income.

"Well, Shirley tell 'e that she din see *de visitors from Red China* again dis mont'." (They both knew who "'e" was).

My twelve-year old brain began working on this bit about Red China, and I put two and two together. I knew, without being told, that Miss Edna and these women would not mind my listening, but that they would resent any questions. I could listen but not interrupt the flow of conversation.

"An' whuh 'e seh?" asked Miss Edna, her mouth setting into a hard, grim line.

"'E ass she how 'e know is he own," replied Miss Ada, sadly, trying to hide the tears surging behind her voice.

Miss Edna exploded.

"Dat son of a bitch! Men can be rail dogs y'know! When deh want somet'ing from yuh, deh busy smellin' rung yuh, an' givin' yuh dis an' givin yuh dat. When deh get it, is hard fuh yuh fuh see dem again."

A calypsonian was belting out "Down on the Bottom Floor" on the *Phillips* radio in Miss Edna's tiny living room while, from a juke box next door, came the smooth, velvety female sounds of "My Tormented Heart" by Sarah Vaughan. A warm northeasterly breeze stirred the pink georgette curtains in the sitting room, made the cheap, yellow and white paper roses on the little coffee table in the living room shiver briefly, and lingered on the pain that was flitting around the warm kitchen. A fly found a drop of blood on the cracked linoleum floor and worked busily on it. A green *gangasaka* sped from under the stained and greasy diocesan church calendar on the wall, chasing another lizard that seemed bent on escape. From the calendar, the Virgin Mary, her skin as pale and smooth as the face in a *Palmolive* advertisement, looked down on us through grease stains with an indifferent Mona Lisa kind of smile. The inscription on the calendar read, "Blessed art thou among women."

"A keep tellin' alyuh dat Shirley behaviour is a abomination unto de Lord. I don' know why she din stay wid de *madam* shi was wid an' learn de lil hairdressin'. When a woman fly in de face uh God's teachin', she will reap de rewards of hell an' damnation, an dat is exac'ly what Shirley gon get. As shore as fate! *Winin'* up sheself half-naked in a den of iniquity! Wha' else alyuh did expec'?"

This was from Miss Ida, Miss Edna's older sister and other black pudding assistant, who had lived with Miss Edna for as long as I could remember and who had found the Lord several years before. She spent every other evening at a little Pentecostal church located in a dwelling house near the train tracks that ran by Miss Edna's house. I never really liked Miss Ida because she was in the habit of reporting me to my mother if she saw me playing cricket on the street with neighborhood children after my parents had left for work. I felt guilty about disliking her because she had saved my life one day when I was five years old and the blow from a donkey cart's too-close revolving wheel had knocked me off the side of a muddy, slippery Lamaha Street into a mossy *trench*, as I walked to school one morning during the rainy season. For several moments, I was unable to recover from the shock of the cold water, or from being in the trench at all; then I started to struggle to hold on to the moss and weeds that grew there, trying desperately to prevent myself from sinking, hating the soggy schoolbook that kept plastering itself to my face and the wet slate that kept getting in my way. It had all happened so quickly that I did not have time to cry out. The cartman, Jaggernauth, did not even realize that he had turned the corner too closely and knocked me off the road into the trench that was swollen after heavy rains. With his cart wheels wobbling and creaking as they rolled slowly away, he proceeded leisurely, flicking his donkey's reins, and singing a popular East Indian song with a cheerful, rhythmic twitch of his head.

I can only recall that my heart seemed to take on new life and that it became the biggest, most active part of my being. It is difficult to describe philosophically, from an adult perspective, what it was like to have nearly drowned at the age of five. The very brevity of my existence up to that point did not allow past events to "flash before my eyes." I simply reacted with the animal instinct to struggle to survive, grabbing at the thin weeds in the trench.

Luckily, Miss Ida had seen it all from a nearby cakeshop where she had been distributing Christian tracts. I later learned that she had cleared the distance between the cakeshop and the trench with an alacrity that belied her usual self-righteous, sober bearing. Even as I began to disappear under the moss and weeds, to feel myself losing consciousness when the muddy water began to flood my lungs, I felt her hands grasping me, dragging me roughly to the roadside, and later turning me over and applying pressure to my lungs.

Miss Edna now paused in her activity and turned her head slowly to take in her sister. Sweat poured from her face, a few drops falling into the black pudding mixture, as she shook her head like a large brown racing mare about to go into the homestretch. One hand was wrapped around the open end of the cow's long intestine fitted on to a tin funnel, and the other grasped the upturned bloody spoon, the handle of which she had been using to force the rice mixture into the *runner*.

"An' who mek *you* God, judge and jury, Ida? Yuh know what it like to live in dese times? Dis is 1958; is not like when we was comin' up. T'ings en cheap nuh mo'. Is na suh easy to get by pun hairdressin' money now. Shirley is a young gyurl, an' she mus' want a few nice t'ings. An' yuh know wha' dey seh—'*woman alone is like tin cup; ev'rybody wan' pass an' dip deh han'.*' *An' to besize,* yuh t'ink is everybody want to deh livin' up in de chu'ch cryin' 'Lord, Lord' like you? Like yuh forgettin' all you use to do in de war years up at de air base *before de spirit ketch yuh!*"

Miss Edna said this with a slightly contemptuous curl of her lip. Miss Ida continued undaunted. She was used to having her self-righteousness derided and had developed the tough hide of an iguana, when it came to attacks on her religiosity.

"All I know is dat if Shirley di' want a few nice t'ings, she got one now. I always seh dat *if yuh mek yuhself grass, goat gun eat yuh.* From de time I hear dat she di' doin' more dan servin' drinks in de Blue Lantern, I feel it was me Christian duty to fin' out whuh was goin' on. Afta rall, she an' Ada is me blood. I hear deh got a private room at de Blue Lantern an all dem big shot Civil Servant an dem does go an watch woman dance half-naked, an' Shirley is one of dese women. I tell y'all dis long ago, but alyuh en' bodduh wid me."

Miss Ida said this with a slight sniff, her bony body seeming to draw in on itself.

The term 'striptease' had not yet entered her lexicon, and I felt a kind of quiet pride in knowing it myself. I had come across it in my furtive, hungry meanderings through "penny-dreadfuls" and American romance magazines that I devoured while locked in the outdoor latrine away from my mother, and by flashlight after everyone else had gone to bed. I used to keep a cache of them stored under my mattress on the top bunk but had to abandon that hiding place after my mother discovered them when one day she had a headache and lay on the bottom bunk to have a rest.

She had seized the lot, including one with a gripping account of a teenage girl in Illinois who was about to be seduced by a stepfather twice her age. For a long time after, I wondered how that story turned out and if the girl eventually told her mother, who had seemed unbelievably dense, about the whole affair which was going on right under her nose.

Miss Ada turned suddenly, furious at Miss Ida's attack on her daughter, sprinkling the flour from her hands and startling the two now blood-gorged flies on the floor.

"Tell me why yuh is such a hypocrite, eh? Yuh know dat dis lil money we mekin' from food an' washin' an' ironin' can barely feed all uh we, *an'* buy clothes *an'* pay rent to. Yuh know dat when rainy season come, an' dis roof start leakin' like a sieve, we miserable because de lan'lord ent fix nutt'n hey in years since we always behin' wid de rent. Yuh know how much people *does tek food pun tick* an' don pay?"

She said this, briefly eyeing Miss Edna who was the most charitable of the trio and glancing meaningfully at me as I quickly polished off the last of a piece of black pudding that Miss Edna had given me. Miss Ida opened her mouth to say something, but Miss Ada quickly and heatedly cut her off.

"When Shirley get dis lil wuk, I t'ink all uh we know wuh was comin' nex'. But almos' ev'ry cent Shirley get, she puttin' in we han'. She makin' good money, an' fuh once we can pay off Bahadur, an' not have to go an' beg 'e fuh rations, an' tell 'e hol' on till nex' week. We can even try an' get dis roof fix weself widdout waitin' pun de stingy dog of a lan'lord. Mr. Cromwell had promise dat 'e will tek care uh Shirley when 'e start followin' she up, an' I t'ink 'e may still do it."

"Yes, but duh was before she had bun in de oven," Miss Ida said drily, picking her teeth with a hairpin.

21

Miss Ada's shoulders sagged, as two large tears slid down her sweat-streaked face.

She wiped them away with a corner of her apron, leaving a bloody pastry smudge in the track of her tears. When she left the Corentyne, she had hoped that she might be able to enroll Shirley in the Carnegie School of Home Economics in Georgetown, but living costs had made that impossible; her children all had to be fed, clothed, housed and educated. There was so much cutting and contriving that you could do in the country to make ends meet. It was not as easy in town. They had all managed so much better in the country when Reggie was alive and worked at the rice mill while she took in washing. After Reggie's death, the mill owners had asked her to vacate the little dilapidated cottage that they had rented to her family for a pittance as a courtesy to Reggie during his lifetime.

Bored by her hairdressing apprenticeship, nauseated by the smell of burning hair, and fatigued by the excessive demands of a short-tempered madam, Shirley had grabbed the opportunity at the Blue Lantern when it arose. Her startling good looks, youth and precocity gave her an intensely sensual appeal. She was an instant favorite at the tavern. Soon she was promoted from bargirl to the main striptease attraction. Then she began coming back to the cottage late at night, reeking of rum, and proudly speaking of the important men in Georgetown who were interested in her and the glowing future they promised. In the three months she had been at the tavern, she was extremely generous to her mother and the other women, even though she was slowly beginning to view them with scorn and near derision. One senior civil servant, James Cromwell, was paying her serious attention, and even though his wife had waited for Shirley one night after the bar closed, and nearly, as Ida had heard, "stripped her naked" on the street, Shirley continued to focus all her romantic attention on him.

"Nevah mine, gyurl," Miss Edna said, placing a hefty arm around Miss Ada's shoulders and being careful not to get any blood on her. "We manage when Reggie dead, an' we gon get t'rough now. *Is not de fuss pickney I mine.*"

Suddenly, I remembered that I had promised to meet my mother at Bahadur's grocery stall in the market to help her with the *goods*. On my way through her living room, I passed Miss Ida's picture of the Holy Trinity. Jesus' benevolent but blank blue eyes followed me out, his white hands extended from his exposed "sacred heart" dripping with blood. I stopped at the front door.

"Miss Edna, my mudduh say to tell yuh dat de las' set uh black puddin' and souse was nice," I called out before I could stop myself. *"Rail* nice."

CHAPTER 4

Sunday afternoons carried with them a regular routine that we broke only if it rained. In my parents' view, children were not supposed to "run about" because of the day's sacredness. Therefore, Bernard and I had to make our play with the Braithwaite children as quiet as possible. Often, however, the Braithwaite children became carried away in their excitement and accustomed lack of parental supervision. Then boys' marble games and girls' *littie* games grew very noisy.

"Who seh you in foursie?" Gwendolyn Braithwaite demanded angrily of me as I tried to slip over to foursie when I thought she was not paying attention to our littie game.

"As far as I concern, you in t'reesie!" she declared emphatically, her voice rising somewhat hysterically as she forgot my mother, who was busy upstairs pounding *fufu* for our midday *breakfast* of split pea soup, cassava, eddoes and dumplings.

My mother had just returned from the Anglican church in the village and changed her "good things" that only saw the light of day when she wore them on a Sunday or other special occasion.

"A tellin' you I in foursie," I insisted. "I been in t'reesie when you went to de pipe to get water."

Gwennie made an angry lunge for her little littie bricks that she had gone to the trouble of selecting near the seawall. The stones there were round and smooth and therefore ideally suited for littie. The scramble for the littie bricks began amidst our yells at each other, and my mother came downstairs. She carefully negotiated her way around the fowl droppings on one of the steps, the belt in one hand, and in the other, the pot spoon dripping with split pea soup.

"You all chirren doan have any respec'?" she demanded, her voice rising above ours, her hand slowly reaching for the belt around her neck. "You all know today is Sunday?"

"Gwennie, go back to yuh yard," she ordered the girl who was already backing away through the gate and out of the yard. "Go back to yuh yard *now!*"

"An' you, Miss Lady, upstairs an' to yuh book, before a give you t'reesie an'foursie," she said, turning to me.

I gingerly edged past her on the backstep, watching her free hand, her face and the belt all at the same time, silently cursing Gwennie, who had taken her littie bricks over to other neighbor friends whose parents were less observing of the Sabbath.

Occasionally when Bernard and Gwennie's brother, Joe-Joe, thought that the other boys in the neighborhood were not looking, they joined in the littie game, and then things would become more boisterous than ever as they tried to beat Gwennie and me at our own game. At other times, Bernard and I sneaked away from our yard and over into the Braithwaites' backyard where, with other neighborhood children, we played hopscotch, skipping games such as "Wedding Cake, Stale Cake," or cricket in the style of "Gedde-Ball-Bowl, Out-A-Man-Bat."

By two in the afternoon, it was time to prepare for Sunday School at three, and then all our earlier exuberance began to fade. Bernard and I bathed, and my mother dressed us in Sunday clothes, socks and shoes after shining our legs with *Vaseline.* All our knee scars from our play with the Braithwaites and others gleamed dully above the black patent leather of our "good shoes." My mother brushed Bernard's hair flat into a tightly coiled, shining mat. She then combed out my hair that she had washed, "plaited fine," and oiled the day before. I hated the torture of having my hair combed out after it was washed and longed to be old enough to go to a madam for a "press and style." Then, I thought, combing my hair would be easier and less painful. Sometimes when my mother combed out my hair after washing it, she had me sit on the floor in front of her while she sat on a chair behind me with my head locked between her knees to keep me from fidgeting. I had to be careful to keep my crying to a minimum, for even while she empathized with my pain, there was a limit to the degree of whining that she would tolerate. At the end of it all, she would have me stand up to face her, carefully inspecting the plaits she had made as if they were her own. Then she would smile in partial self-congratulation and say to me, "Look at my nice gyurl!" Momentarily, that remark would seem to make all the discomfort I had just endured worthwhile. It did not, however, reduce the painful impact of photographs of black female models in *Ebony* and *Tan* magazines. Their straight, smooth, gleaming, black satin-looking hair seemed to me, at that time, to speak of real grace and beauty.

My father took no part in these Sunday preparations since he felt that these were my mother's duties, an assumption that she did not dispute. He merely took up his position in the Berbice chair, his face hidden behind the *Sunday Chronicle*. Just before we left, he emerged to give us money for the collection. Then they saw us off into the sweltering Sunday afternoon heat on our way to the village Catholic Church. One condition of my mother's being able to marry my Roman Catholic father in 1946 was her agreement with the Church's stipulation that her children be reared as Catholics. My father himself rarely attended mass, but he would demand a detailed explanation from my mother if we ever missed Sunday School.

"Who made you?"

"God made me."

"Why did God make you?"

"To know Him, to love Him, to serve Him, and to be happy with Him in this world and forever in the next."

The Sunday School children droned on in response to the nun's questions from the catechism. The air was so hot and thick that I felt it moving around my face, down my neck and inside the socks that Grammudduh crocheted for my last birthday. They were already too tight, and the hard cotton thread was beginning to leave a crotchet pattern on my skin. Often, my attention strayed to the statues of the saints, cold, indifferent looking even in that hot church, all alabaster white with no eyeballs and dead outstretched hands like Fogarty's show window dolls.

Bernard fell asleep, made drowsy by the heat, and tired out from a morning of "bat-and-ball." His head dropping onto my shoulder, he lapsed into an adenoidal snore. The nun prodded him awake amid the titters of our Sunday School classmates, too intimidated by the solemn atmosphere of the church to be more mischievous. She interrogated him about the difference between original sin and mortal sin, the sacraments, the definition of Extreme Unction, questions that interested him little. Mother Camille warned him of the danger he ran of not being able to take his First Communion and (God forbid!) to make his confirmation—indeed the danger his indifference posed to his immortal soul. When the collection plate came around, Bernard and I often withheld the two pennies that my father had given each of us. At the end of Sunday School, we used them to buy "chip" or "grate" *sugar-cake* and *genips* from the woman who had set up her tray outside the church. We vowed to each other to confess this sin to Father Adonis when we said our next confession. During the period when I waited for the results of the scholarship, I prayed that God would not seek revenge for this slap in His face by ensuring that I did not pass. After Sunday School, Bernard and I carefully checked each other's face for any telltale fragments of sugar cake and turned the corner into Lamaha Street with the gravity of the righteous.

Another important feature of Sunday afternoon was our bike rides through the nearby suburb of Subryanville where some of area's more well off lived. After returning home to an afternoon snack of my mother's sponge cake and mauby or ginger beer, Bernard and I changed our clothes and rode madly through Subryanville, racing each other, letting go of the handlebars and doing all sorts of stunts that would have made my mother apoplectic with rage. One Sunday afternoon, we happened to pass a court in Subryanville where four men were playing tennis. As we made one of our swift, wind-driven rides past them, we heard the soft thud of tennis balls on the court and the men's muffled calls to each other as they kept score. Tennis and cars were not part of the social life of Lamaha Street, and we paid little attention to the game as we cavorted on the street outside. Just as we passed the cars for about the third time, a tennis ball shot out onto the street in front of Bernard. Taken by surprise, he swerved suddenly to avoid it and, in doing so, ran sidewise into a shiny black *Morris* car parked by the roadside. The collision knocked him off the bike, and he lay sprawled in Subryanville's dust, his ten-year old face a picture of pathetic bewilderment. He was bleeding from a cut alongside his left eye, and his knuckles and knees were badly scraped. The bicycle lay on the street, its wheels spinning. The car sported a long silvery scrape and dent like a gleaming scar along its side, the result of the impact of the handlebar and pedals.

The noise of the accident brought the four tennis players rushing from the court to the scene of the accident. One East Indian and three light-skinned men, they were resplendent in their tennis whites. They moved immediately to the car, ignoring Bernard whom I was trying to retrieve from the dust.

"My God! Look what you've done to the justice's cah!" said one of the light-skinned men, fairly bristling with anger and slightly sweaty from the game.

Perspiration moved in slow tiny trickles down his face behind his glasses like rivulets of rain on Kitty's muddy roads. He ran a finger along the offending scrape as though hoping that, by some miracle, he could work a kind of mechanical healing. He looked at another of the light-skinned players, a burly freckled man, trying to enlist his supporting rage against Bernard who had by this time barely managed to wobble to his feet.

"Can your parents replace a car like this young man?" the hefty man inquired angrily as he advanced threateningly.

He grabbed the bleeding Bernard by the collar and shook him till his teeth rattled and the blood coursed down his cheek and into the side of his mouth.

"Well, can they?" he bellowed, looking from one to the other of us, his colour becoming an ugly, hot pink. I shrank from him, hoping secretly that he would be satisfied with Bernard as the sacrificial lamb on his altar of rage. His eyes were a clear, hard blue, and I had the uneasy feeling that these were probably what God's eyes looked like when Bernard and I misused our collection money.

Late at night when we children were in bed, I had sometimes overheard my parents' conversation, as they sat in the moonlight on the little landing at the top of our front steps. Sometimes they reminisced about their unpleasant encounters with colonial government administrators, many of them English, or their local English-educated offspring. I heard the hushed tones with which my mother (who was not often intimidated by anyone) referred to Matron Douglas, a dreaded local white woman who ran the city hospital. The Matron's father had been a well-off sugar planter, and she was the scourge of any young nurse who dared to slack off on the gruelling twelve-hour shifts during the forties when alternative employment opportunities for working class Guianese women were few and poor.

Once, I overheard my father reminisce about the two long years it had taken for him to get his back-pay after he had been demobilized from the British Royal Army Medical Corps in 1946. In the course of two years, he made repeated fruitless trips to the Colonial Secretary's Office as he was bounced from one government bureaucracy to another. He had even visited the Anglican archbishop's office, perhaps hoping that this dignitary's closeness to the twin deities in the church and the local colonial office would lead to a successful intercession. Finally, in 1948, after Bernard's birth and several unanswered letters to the governor, my father had demanded to see this illusive and illustrious personage. Our family was growing, and as a poorly paid junior officer in the government, my father had needed the money desperately. He therefore used his lunch periods to camp out for weeks in the outer office of the governor's personal secretary. Sitting on the hard public bench there, he had endured the contemptuous glances of colonial government officers who went about their business, perhaps vaguely wondering why this bespectacled twenty-eight-year old Black man (who just three years previously, might have been called upon to give his life for their motherland) did not just give up and go home. At last, several weeks after this, the governor agreed to see him and my father finally received his back pay.

Standing outside that tennis court in Subryanville in the hot Sunday sun, watching my brother manhandled and staring into those blue eyes, cold, flat and dead like those of the white dolls in Fogarty's, I felt for the first time a keen sense of my parents' pain.

"You people have no respect for property," the judge hissed.

"Here it is, your parents have simply left you to run like wild animals through the streets. I am going to hold on to this bicycle, and you go home and tell whomever it is you live with to come and see me here at the court if they want it back."

With that, he grabbed the bicycle that was lying on the ground, and the four men all made their way back to the tennis court. My mother's damaged bike squealed protestingly and moved haltingly like an unwilling child as the judge wheeled and tugged it back to the court. Occasionally, one or other of the men glared at us over his retreating shoulder or muttered something nasty about uncontrolled ragamuffins. Bernard could no longer contain himself, and he sobbed miserably as we trudged disconsolately back home where we found my mother alone getting dinner.

She was too alarmed at Bernard's condition to give us both the whipping that we would certainly have gotten under other circumstances. As we told her of the judge's treatment of Bernard and his declaring her bicycle a ward of the tennis court, her face tightened in silent anger. She hurriedly dressed Bernard's wounds and left for the tennis court since her bicycle was her only means of conveyance to work. Moreover, she was also anxious to give the judge a piece of her mind over his treatment of Bernard.

When my mother returned, she gave us the following account of her meeting with the judge and the others at the court.

"I am the boy's mother," she told the judge, without bothering to elaborate further on her identity or who "the boy" was.

She had been, as she recounted to us, *breathing short* because of her anger over Bernard's treatment, the seizure of her bike, and her fast walk to Subryanville.

"Madam, I am Justice Day," the judge said, "and your son has scraped my car. I hope you are prepared to make some form of restitution, or I shall have to hold this bicycle."

The judge's friends stood around in a tight little circle, eyeing my mother censoriously.

"You all don' have any feelin's? You all coun' see dat he was bleedin'? You behave as dough your kyar more important dan a chile. Mister, you doan have chirren?" she demanded angrily.

My mother and her friends felt that the condition of childlessness left one prone to unfeeling treatment of children. In this, she ignored the times when she herself and other mothers in the neighborhood were most unsparing of the strap for some of the most minor childhood infractions.

She was already familiar with Justice Day because 'Gatha, our dressmaker, had once taken her child-father to court for child support, and Justice Day, then Magistrate Day, had seemed very lax in enforcing the payments, asking the timid 'Gatha if she had not thought about the possibility of having to run down Eustace for support when she had engaged in (as Day had snidely put it) "wanton dalliance" with him. Sitting in the spectator area of the steamy court room where she had gone to give 'Gatha moral support, my mother had fairly bristled at this. She and 'Gatha had left the courtroom after the hearing, quietly calling Magistrate Day a "red devil" and consigning him and Eustace to hell. Further enraged by these recollections, my mother took firm hold of the bicycle handlebars.

"An' to t'ink you have de gall to call yuhself a judge! Hol'in on to people property an' maltreatin' deh chirren! You all does t'ink po' people ent got feelin's, but if my husban' was here you woulda know. I know where yuh office is in de Victoria Law Courts on High Street. I live at eighty-three Lamaha Street, Kitty, an' when you fin' out how much it is to fix yuh kyar, contac' me dere an' leh me know, an' I will get de money to you." (At this time in Kitty, few, but the very important, had telephones). With some conviction, my mother had declared her intention to pay, but it was, in reality, an expense that had given her pause. Justice Day drew breath to speak, but before he could say anything more, she had snatched the bicycle angrily out of his grasp and walked swiftly away. The judge and his friends looked on open-mouthed.

While my mother was gone, my father returned from his monthly Sunday meeting at the British Guiana Legion. When he removed the dressing from the cut beside Bernard's eye, he anticipated that there might be scarring when the cut healed. Also, to avoid the delay of the uncertain possibility of transportation for the trip to the hospital, he decided, using his own nursing and dispensing experience, to stitch the cut himself. Needless to say, Bernard was initially most unwilling and uncooperative at the prospect of this kind of domestic medical care. His screams rose at the thought of stitches, but my father was undaunted. He proceeded to scrub and wash a pot, boil water, and put on my mother's rubber gloves over which he had poured hot water. While he boiled a sewing needle and cotton thread, he advanced towards Bernard who knew better than to anger him by any further displays of recalcitrance. Next my father cleaned the cut thoroughly, washed his gloved hands again with hot water, and sewed the edges of the cut together in much the same way that Miss Seegobin in my sewing class at school had taught us to do overstitching of two edges of a piece of cloth. The cut was quite close to Bernard's eye, and my father had to be careful that Bernard's sudden movements did not cause the needle to injure his eye. He yelled every time the needle pierced skin along the edges of the cut, but he tried to remain still because my father had explained to him why he needed to close the cut.

The Braithwaites and a few other children in the neighborhood had heard that Bernard's father was going to "stitch his face." Drawn by his screams, they congregated on our back steps in the gathering gloom of that Sunday evening. My father, who did not share my mother's unmindfulness about having some of his actions observed by the neighborhood children, immediately ordered them home, slammed the backdoor shut, and continued with the operation. In response to my father's curt dismissal, the Braithwaites and other children who had gathered on the steps later nicknamed Bernard "Patches."

In a few days the cut had healed in a thin, almost threadlike line, and my father later snipped away the stitches. Today, nearly forty years later, what remains of the scar is barely perceptible. What has been more lasting, however, is the nickname. Bernard now lives in New York, and on the rare occasion when he has heard someone call out, "Patches" on a snow-blown street, he knows that it is a Lamaha Street voice of forty shadows past. Then he remembers that hot, painful, far Sunday evening when he took courage and joined his father in a communion of trust.

CHAPTER 5

One rainy Saturday morning, sounds of loud laughter made us all rush to the front window of the cottage to see what was happening on Lamaha Street. Groups of neighborhood children and a few adults—some women on the way to the market and men going about other business—stood along the grassy sides of the street, some holding their stomachs, doubled over with laughter. The street was a kind of liquid *puttah puttah*, like a thick *Ovaltine* milk shake. Mr. Braithwaite was drunk, and his walk up the street to his house was impeded by his bicycle and guttering materials. He ambled unsteadily from one side of the road to the other, slipping and sliding. At some points, he seemed to mark time in the mud only to have both legs skid sideways away from his bicycle as he tried to keep both hands on the handlebars. He then went seat first into the mud, his bicycle skittering away with loud clangs. He would get up and then try to mount the bicycle, only to go crashing into the puttah puttah again to the sounds of shrieking laughter from the onlookers along the roadside. After all these fruitless efforts, he got on allfours, crawling sideways like a crab towards the bicycle, as his legs again slid out from under him. Again more raucous laughter from the slowly growing groups of bystanders. By that time, after one of his falls, the bicycle handlebars had cut his temple, and one elbow was scraped from a slide along the ground. Rufus the Rice-eater, attracted by the laughter, began yapping at him, running into the muddy street and making sudden threatening charges at his trouser leg. A thick, brown ooze covered his khaki work clothes. Bored by the monotony of their own lives, not wishing to be denied the opportunity of the amusement he provided, and not wanting to relinquish the relatively clean safety of the grassy sides of the road, none of the spectators lifted a finger to help him.

Bernard and I were eager to leave the cottage to get a better view of the spectacle, but my mother prevented us. She herself would occasionally peak out at Mr. Braithwaite's predicament, sometimes trying to hide her own amusement, but often muttering in sympathy about "poor Mrs. Braithwaite" and the embarrassment she must be feeling. The Braithwaite children, who were devoted and often unsympathetic spectators of the whippings and other parental humiliations of other neighborhood children, were indoors viewing their father's disgrace from behind the cracks in their windows.

Eventually, Mr. Braithwaite tried the tactic of crawling through the mud in the style of the commandos we had seen in war movies shown at the village's "Hollywood" cinema. It seemed that, in his drunken desperation, he had decided to abandon his bike altogether. The sweat trickling down his mud-splattered face, he crawled to the side of the road in an effort to avoid Rufus and the mud. For support, he then tried to grab hold of a female-onlooker's skirt. She immediately whacked his hand with the ragged umbrella she was carrying.

"Look, get away from me, you ol' *rumsucker* you, you ol' *VanDrunkenburg!*" she cried, snatching her skirt from his hand, as she, too, nearly lost her footing at the side of the road. Again more side-splitting laughter from the spectators. The woman's belligerence gave Rufus the idea that it was open season on Mr. Braithwaite, and, growling ferociously, he lunged this time not just at Mr. Braithwaite's trouser leg but at his bare ankle. This only added to the general amusement as Mr. Braithwaite and the dog tussled in the mud.

Unable to bear watching her father being torn apart in this way, Gwennie Braithwaite ran barefoot from their house, threw a brick at Rufus, and chased him off.

Rufus, whose courage was reserved for the passing milkman and helpless persons like Mr. Braithwaite, was terrified of the neighbourhood children, who often found amusement in tormenting stray dogs by pelting them mercilessly. Rufus ran off immediately, and Gwennie tearfully bent down, took her father's arm, and gingerly negotiated him out of the mud, trying desperately to hold on to him as he swung his arms towards the onlookers and muttered angry, slurred profanities. Following this incident, her husband's drunken violence was increasingly extended to her and their children, and Mrs. Braithwaite became an even more shadowy figure.

After he had taken time out from his rounds to enjoy the spectacle of Mr. Braithwaite's progress up the street, the newspaper deliverer finally arrived at our gate. He threw the *Daily Chronicle* carelessly onto our front steps, and because we were all so engrossed in Mr. Braithwaite's predicament, we barely noticed the paper until Bernard nearly tripped over it some hours later. I picked it up, momentarily forgetting the scholarship results that we had looked for so fruitlessly in the past. I turned the pages to find out what had happened in the latest comic strip episode of "Mandrake the Magician" and saw the headline of the second page—"Government County Scholarship Results."

I felt my heart beat faster and my hands go moist as my eyes ran up and down the page to find the name of my school. I saw the names of the city-student winners from schools like Smith's Church Congregational, Broad Street Government, and St. George's Anglican. At first, in my panicky haste, I did not see my school, and then there it was, and below it—my name. The first time I had ever seen it in print. For a few seconds I checked its spelling, stunned. Here at last was the open door that so many Guianese parents feverishly sought for their children. Suddenly, I understood the significance of the harsh experience of Mr. Isaac Davis' scholarship class, his coldly regulated cruelty, the unending hours of fractions and decimal points, and the interminable rote learning of the Intelligence Test section of the examination.

I had a great sense of the weight of my parents' sacrifice. I remembered the pelting rain on the day of the scholarship examination when my mother had ridden her bicycle from Kitty to Georgetown, arriving drenched at the examination center at St. George's Anglican School on Church Street. She brought me lunch because she did not want me to risk illness by going out to nearby Fogarty's or Booker's as we had originally planned. Later, with trembling fingers, she stuffed two *Halls* mints into my blue school uniform pocket and returned to Kitty in the driving rain. I remembered the quiet confidence of the young city scholarship-takers.

The year before, Steven Osbourne had done so well in the examination that he had been given a special scholarship by the Kitty Local Authority. Just before the scholarship examination, he had begun to come down with a debilitating fever, later diagnosed as malaria. That had been his last chance to take the examination, since, the next year, he would have passed the age limit. Steven was one of Kitty's best and brightest. He was the second of seven, and his father was a carpenter at Sandbach Parker, the city shipping firm near the great Demerara River. Often on payday, Mrs. Osbourne (Miss Oz, as we called her) would have to get dressed and make the hot, tedious bus trip to the city to get hold of part of her husband's pay before he and his workmates could hit the rumshops in Tiger Bay after work. The hub of Osbourne home life was the hot kitchen where food preparation for the next meal would begin on the iron wood stove almost as soon as the last meal was over. Or where Miss Oz would be sweating over a scrubbing board in a tub full of her husband's stubborn khakis and the children's clothes. On the day of the scholarship examination, she had *nineted* the shivering Steven with *Vicks Vaporub*, dressed him in his khaki school uniform, wrapped him in a blanket, and together they had boarded the yellow Kitty Regent bus to go down to the examination center. On the journey, she had hovered protectively over the sick boy, *sapping* him with *Limacol*, hating herself because she knew that he should have been in bed, but sure that in later years he would prove to be her ticket out of the drudgery and poverty that slowly consumed her life. Many people on the bus knew their circumstances and that this was the day of the scholarship exam. Therefore when Leon, the bus driver, generously waived their fare, no one on the bus had demurred. Some mothers among the passengers suggested remedies to Mrs. Osbourne for Steven's condition, including a "good cleaning out" with a bush purgative after the exam. They felt certain that his "blood mussie dirty," a clear indication of biliousness. In spite of his illness, Steven had shot a look of hatred at the donor of this advice that he knew would only increase his discomfort.

"Walk good, Miss Oz. Walk good Steven. Kill dem dead boy!" Leon had called, as mother and son got off the bus. Miss Oz waited all day at her sister's cakeshop near the city examination center in order to minister to Stephen during the lunch break.

Steven had been one of Mr. Davis' "promising pupilss." As such, he was greatly favored and rarely subjected to the torment Mr. Davis inflicted on the other students, but this made him the butt of envy and retaliatory cruelty from many of Mr. Davis' young victims. One day, his worn out school shoes had finally come apart, and, never one to keep her children from their education because of such a trivial occurrence, Miss Oz had gotten out a black pair of her own shoes that were laced up in front like a man's, but narrower and slightly heeled. She announced that Steven would wear them the next day. Even though he felt revulsion at the prospect, he did not dare to object because Miss Oz maintained strict control over her children and did not brook even the mildest of protestations against her orders. The next morning, Steven left home for school at the latest time possible to avoid coming into contact with the Braithwaites and others. In order to hide his shoes, he walked on the grassy roadside all the way to school. Then, he hurried into the building in the last wave of late-comers, too preoccupied with avoiding Mr. Davis' "Little Nell" to look down at his shoes. All day he remained at his desk, even eating his lunch there with his feet tucked under it.

In the afternoon, he waited until he thought everyone had left, but as he turned into Lamaha Street, the boys who had already gotten home were just beginning a game of cricket on the street. Pursued swiftly by Joe-Joe Braithwaite, the ball rolled onto the grassy roadside and stopped at Steven's feet. Joe-Joe bent to retrieve the ball and turned away, to Steven's relief. Then, Joe-Joe stopped as though he had just remembered something. He turned, looked down at Steven's feet, and broke out into a loud triumphant peel of laughter.

"O God, 'e wearin' high heels now! You all come an' see!" Joe-Joe cried to the batsman, wicket-keeper and bowler who were impatient because Fine T'ings, the thin, underweight batsman, was going for his second run while Joe-Joe delayed throwing the ball to the wicket-keeper.

Pointing to Steven's feet, Joe-Joe began to double up with laughter. The batsman stopped running and came over, along with the others, while Steven stood ashamed and rooted to the grassy spot. They began to pull him out onto the roadway, pointing to his shoes, and beginning a slow laugh that gradually became side-splitting.

"So how t'ings going, Miss Osbourne?" scoffed Fine T'ings, thumping the edge of his bat on the road as he bent over laughing.

"When Miss Oz gun gi' yuh she dress?" asked Bruck-Up, the wicket-keeper, who was left with a limp after being hit by a dray cart on another Kitty road where, two years before, he had been playing cricket. His broken leg had been badly set and had not healed straight.

Laughing uncontrollably, they encircled him and joined in song with Winston, the bowler and Joe-Joe's brother. They began the words of the children's folksong:

> "Dere's a colored gyurl in the ring
> Tra la la la la
> Dere's a colored gyurl in the ring
> Tra la la la la
> Dere's a colored gyurl in the ring
> Tra la la la la
> For she like sugar and I like plum"

Riddled with shame, Steven tore away from them, and they gave chase, joined by Rufus the Rice Eater and other dogs.

That year, when the results of the scholarship were announced in the *Daily Chronicle*, Steven had "topped the colony." Miss Oz had been preparing to go down to Sandbach Parker to effect the usual retrieval of her husband's pay packet. Instead, she stayed home to bake Steven his own little loaf of bread, and at breakfast, she gave him a boiled egg all for himself. Throughout the day, people came to the Osbourne home to congratulate Miss Oz and Steven. ("So wha' yuh gun be now boy? Docta?"). Some women brought little bowls of food, and Miss Edna sent over black pudding by Miss Ida who prayed over Steven. ("Lord keep 'im in a straight an' righteous path, an' never let 'im forget 'is mudduh in 'er trials and tribulations"). Leon repeated to everyone on the bus that it was he who had driven Steven to the examination. ("Is dis same same bus 'e de guh dung wid you know. An' 'e de sick sick"). Momentarily forgetting his earlier remonstrations to Miss Oz about all the goods she "de tek pun tick" without paying, Bahadur, the market grocer, arrived in the evening with a bar of *Cadbury's Hazelnut Chocolate* "fuh de lil scholar." The next morning, Balgobin, the milkman, brought Miss Oz free extra milk because "yuh know, Miss Oz, milk good fuh chirren brains." That Friday night Mr. Osbourne came home sober with his pay intact for the first time in years.

A few days later, Steven's church confirmation photograph appeared in the *Daily Chronicle* above an article headed, "Kitty Lad Tops Colony in Government County Scholarship Exam." The article referred to Steven's tutelage under "Mr. Isaac Davis, now well-known for his creditable and untiring efforts in acquiring scholarship successes." The writer of the article described Steven as "the son of Mr. Cuthbert Osbourne, Sandbach Parker carpenter, and Mrs. Osbourne." Later, Miss Oz pawned a pair of gold bangles that she had long held in reserve, and with the proceeds and money she had been able to hide away from Mr. Osbourne, she bought Steven a second-hand *Raleigh* bicycle, his school uniform and books. When the new term began, Steven went to the country's leading boys' secondary school in Georgetown. We would often see him riding through Lamaha Street in his new uniform—short khaki pants, white shirt with yellow and black striped tie, cap with the school's emblem, and brown shoes with white socks. His bottom swivelled from side to side on the saddle as he struggled with the pedals' down-strokes on the adult gents *Raleigh* bike. Now Joe-Joe, Winston, Fine T'ings and Bruck-Up ignored him entirely. These barefoot boys would stop their game of cricket and silently let him pass. It was like they felt that he now belonged to a world completely foreign to their own. In his stare at the road ahead, there was a lonely fixedness. I wondered if he missed the boys' former attention, negative though it was. I wondered too about the alienating power of this world to which he had gained admission against impossible odds, a world waiting now to claim me.

I ran to my mother with the newspaper.

"Mama! Mama! Look! A pass! A pass!"

She snatched the newspaper from my grasp, showering flour all over me and the paper. Saturday was her baking day, and she had been kneading dough in the kitchen, her hands up past her wrists in flour. She screamed for my father who was in the yard, and together they bent over the paper.

"Boy, it look like she get it in trute," she said to my father through tears and then suddenly clasped me to her bosom.

My father tried to contain himself, but I could feel the tremor in his voice as he said slowly, not trusting the printed word that he read over and over, "Yes, yes. It look like she railly mek it." Bernard ran down the front steps to go over to the Braithwaite children to give them the news.

There was a knock on the door. It was Mr. Davis. My mother quickly retired to the kitchen to wash her hands, while my father deferentially invited him to have a seat in the living room.

"Well, I see you all have gotten the results. I came to congratulate the girl." (Mr. Davis still could not say my name).

"It seems that she has topped the colony in the English Language portion of the exam," he continued. "But her mark in Arithmetic is the lowest of those who passed. It appears that fractions continue to be her bugbear."

He gave me a reproving look as he said this, and I tried to look appropriately downcast and chastised, while thinking, "At leas' A will never have to see *you* again."

By this time, my mother had gone to the chiffonier, brought out her good snap glasses and filled them with wine.

"Would you have a little drink with us to celebrate?" my father asked him. (My father always reverted to Standard English when dealing with the educated and professional classes).

Sipping the wine, Mr. Davis continued, "She will now be entering the leading government secondary school for girls. I hope you are all aware of what an important step this is, and I hope that she makes the best of this opportunity. She will now be competing with the brightest, and I hope that she will be equal to it."

He said this last sentence eyeing me sternly over his bifocals.

"You doan worry Mr. D. I will be watching her," my mother said, putting enough of a warning into her glance at me to let me know that she was serious and at the same time to assure Mr. Davis.

In 1958, Balgobin's niece, Drupattie, Manuel Gomes and I were the only scholarship recipients at our school. In spite of Mr. Davis' grimly implied predictions about the inattentive Manuel's future occupation in a salt goods shop, the boy had given a good account of himself in the examination. Mr. Davis had hoped that Manuel's parents, whose home he had just visited, would send him to the leading boys' secondary school. Instead, being devout Catholics, they had decided to send their son to the colony's Jesuit secondary school on *Brickdam* in the city.

So I was now to embark on a new adventure. Mr. Davis' admonitions about sustained high academic performance went in one of my twelve-year old ears and out the other. I was more concerned with the prospect of wearing the coveted green uniform of the city's leading secondary school to which many were called and few were chosen. I saw myself riding down Camp Street with new friends all clad in green, all speaking Standard English, and all referring occasionally to "Mummy and Daddy." I looked forward to playing hockey, tennis and netball, games which were light years removed from, what seemed to me then, the crude village schoolyard games of "catcher," "bat-and-ball" and "Coloured Girl in the Ring."

CHAPTER 6

It was late August, a hot, dry dusty midday. Few ventured out, and no one played cricket in the street at times like these when even the north-east trade winds brought little relief to a village baking like bread in a bright charcoal oven. Yet my mother was determined that she and I would go to 'Gatha's so that I would have the final fitting of my school uniform before school began the next week. From inside our house, as my mother was getting out her umbrella to shade us on our way, we heard the sound of "clippety clops." These were not the sounds of a dray cart, nor were they those of some anaemic stray animal running wild through the village street. These were light, harnessed, regulated "clippeties" and "cloppeties," sounds of a well-fed, well-groomed animal. My mother and I looked out the window.

The Black leader of the country's political opposition was riding through the village. Just over thirty, he was about six feet, two inches tall, with low cropped hair and a neatly trimmed moustache. He reminded me of pictures I had seen in my mother's book of British royal family photographs that showed King George VI and his entourage engaged in a royal hunt near Sandringham or some such English-sounding estate. The opposition leader wore a black, peaked riding cap, white open-necked shirt, beige riding breeches, and shining, black, high-topped riding boots. The trappings on his horse jangled lightly as he rode along the dusty Lamaha Street. Even the stray dogs seemed to know that this was not the common dray behind which they could run and yappingly torment. Rufus growled and then slunk away, his head and tail down, almost apologetically. The Chief, as his admirers called him, sat erect, bobbing up from the saddle, his back straightening and his chest thrusting out rhythmically with the trotting movement of the horse. A phrase that I had once heard from a source I could not then recall kept running through my mind: "Mad dogs and Englishmen go out in the noonday sun." I started to say it aloud to the rhythm of the hoof beats, and my mother advanced towards me threateningly with her umbrella. Like many of the village women, including Miss Edna who made black pudding for the Chief's party fund-raisers, my mother took pride in the Chief's leadership and was active in his party's women's political auxilliary, baking sponge cakes and cassava pone for various social events that the party organized in the village.

Many of the other Black villagers also had great love and respect for the opposition leader, whom many of them called *Kabaka*, the Bugandan translation of the word "King." Like Stephen Osbourne, the "Kabaka" or Chief was a "Kitty boy" and had also been educated at the leading boys' secondary school where he had won the prestigious Guiana Scholarship and then gone on to study law in London. Following graduation, he had returned to the colony in the late forties, taken up practice as a barrister-at-law, and entered politics. Along with a young, Guianese dentist of East Indian descent, the Chief then became joint leader of a party that had the overwhelming support of the combined Black and East Indian popular majority. After their party won the 1953 national elections with a resounding popular victory, the two co-leaders became members of an Executive Council to whom the British government granted control of Guiana's internal government. The political premiership of the country also then went to the East Indian dentist, the founder of the national political movement. However, the British governor still remained in overall political control, with matters of external affairs and other specific areas of government remaining under the English colonial administration.

But this was an uneasy partnership between the local and expatriate members of the national government. The Chief and the East Indian premier had been vociferous and impatient in their calls for full national independence while drawing attention to the Guianese masses' deplorable living conditions under the colonial government. In the capital in 1953, there were political protest marches against the British administration, and these had ended in the arrest of many demonstrators. At that time a tool of the colonial master class, the *Daily Chronicle* had reported in spit press fashion on September 13, 1953 that "it had been suggested in certain quarters that members of the Executive Council had gone to the sugar estates demanding that sugar workers should strike, and that there were certain unions, controlled by ministers of the government, awaiting orders to show their sympathy in similar fashion." Furthermore, the British were uneasy about the specter of communism that seemed to haunt the outdoor protest rallies of the young bow-tied East Indian politician-dentist. He urged the largely responsive local working people to recognize the brotherhood they shared with many of the colonial and other dispossessed around the world.

Fearful of such political recalcitrance in a colony that had hitherto proved to be governable in spite of poor social and economic conditions, the British government hastily recalled their "gift" of internal self-government. The British suspended the Constitution in late 1953 and declared a state of emergency, with the colony reverting to direct British rule. British troops arrived in the country to restore order. Some members of the former Executive Council, including the East Indian premier, were detained by the British, and a state of emergency was imposed. The Chief, who had been Party Chairman and Minister of Education during the period of internal self-government, was not among local politicians who were taken into custody. The British then put in place an interim government made up of trusted local politicians under their own close supervision.

By 1955, the racial unity forged during the early fifties between the Black Chief and the East Indian leader had begun to unravel, and the Chief broke away to form his own party. With cries of *Apaan Jhat* being sounded, popular support for each of these leaders was divided along sharp racial lines. In 1957, the East Indian leader defeated the Chief to assume the premiership in newly held elections when the British again reinstituted internal self-government. Racial division had now made the colony safer for British rule.

On this hot midday in 1958, the Chief reined in at Mr. Jacobs' corner cakeshop to have a glass of cold mauby, a local fermentation tasting somewhat like beer. Mr. Jacobs always felt that it was a privilege to give the Chief a free glass, and before handing it to him, he would carefully wipe the rim of the glass with the cotton rag he kept for this purpose under the counter. Some months before, while I was in the shop buying butter-flaps, I witnessed one of the Chief's visits at close range. A few village men began to gather around, tipping their hats deferentially to him, wiping their sweating foreheads with the backs of their hands and asking, "How yuh do, sah?" or "How t'ings goin' wid de guvment?" To show his fellowship with the working people, the Chief would call them by name, making inquir-

ies in Creolese about some personal aspect of their lives—
"How nuh Elroy? Dat gyurl yuh livin wid, she get de baby
yet? Is hummuch pickney yuh got now? Hummuch dis
one mek?" Or he would turn to old Mr. Padmore who had
retired from the Water Works as a night watchman.

"Suh wha' hapnin' Daddy Pads? Dem people still gie'in'
yuh hell fuh get de lil pension?"

I had heard the men ask him how he felt about losing
the election. He replied, "Black people still got to learn to
support deh own. We still like we in de crab barrel, man,
climin' pun one anodda back, tryin' to tear one anodda dung
suh we weself could get up. All I got fuh tell alyou is dat if
we doan win de nex' election, *kyat eat alyou dinner."*

'Gatha was expecting her third child by Eustace, a young
local policeman. Child-bearing had left her fat in a soft,
puffy, somewhat unhealthy sort of way, and her breathing
was laboured and audible as she pedalled away, sweating,
at the *Singer* sewing machine in the corner of the little living room. Her two young children were under the house
playing with neighborhood friends, and Eustace was in
the single bedroom of the cottage sleeping through the heat.

After about five years of repeated promises to marry
'Gatha and support his children, Eustace had finally agreed
to the former, and this had made 'Gatha ecstatic. She felt
that a change in her social status from *child-mother* to respectable wife and mother would miraculously make all
things right and that after their marriage, Eustace would
forget his other women, become more loving towards her
and the children, and support them all. She conveniently
forgot the times when, in her legal efforts to secure child-
support from him, she had had to face the scoffing Magistrate Day and the smilingly smug Eustace in the courtroom.
She shoved aside thoughts of past instances when, as though

she were the offending party, she endured the humiliation of Day's barrage of faintly hostile questions regarding her relationship with Eustace. The colonial administration had no wish to encourage flagrant law-breaking, but the officials had an even stronger desire not to antagonize local policemen like Eustace who were responsible for enforcing the law and who were the critical element in many legal confrontations between the government and individual members of the British Guianese masses.

Therefore, while the presiding magistrate often ostensibly admonished Eustace to support his children, the question of whether or not he actually fulfilled this legal obligation was a matter of indifference to the courts.

In addition, Eustace had at least two other child-mothers, one of whom had threatened to tear 'Gatha apart when she went shopping in the Kitty market one Saturday morning. Eustace was as delinquent in his responsibilities to these other women and their children as he was to 'Gatha and hers. Yet 'Gatha was the only one of his women who would defy the possibility of a subsequent beating by him and take him to court. Sometimes Eustace spent time at the other women's homes, explaining his absences to 'Gatha by saying that he had been called out of town on official police business. Largely, he lived off his own income and the little these women were able to generate, and was known to be violently jealous, beating them mercilessly if he thought that some other man had entered the picture. He had the stature of a welterweight boxer and was greatly feared by the criminals in the village lock-ups who came into his "custody." Woe betide the petty thief who, in the course of his arrest, offered Eustace resistance. Invariably, this wretch would arrive at the station lock-ups wishing that he had kept his furtive hands out of the fowl coop near which he had been discovered at four o'clock that rainy morning.

When my mother and I arrived at 'Gatha's cottage for my school uniform fittings, four of her female relatives were sitting, fanning themselves, around the sewing machine that she pedalled. They were quietly discussing general preparations for 'Gatha's upcoming marriage and the styles of the bridesmaids' dresses. The women regarded 'Gatha, as the prospective bride, with new respect, even though they all knew that the future of the proposed marriage was in serious question. 'Gatha was six months pregnant, and her large belly occupied all the space between her chair and the edge of the sewing table. Eventually, the women left, and she turned her attention to my mother and her requirements regarding the uniforms. As 'Gatha took my measurements, she and my mother spoke in lowered tones so as not to wake the sleeping Eustace, whose loud snores reverberated through the warm cottage.

"Suh how come 'e change 'e mine sudden-sudden suh?" my mother whispered to her, glad that the women had left and that she now had 'Gatha all to herself.

"A decide to tek t'ings in han'," 'Gatha replied in an even lower whisper, glancing furtively at the bedroom door, and reaching both arms around me with the tape measure. "A decide to go an' see Mama Rose."

Mama Rose was the village obeah woman, and it was whispered that many a slippery prospective bridegroom had been forced to see the light after her supernatural ministrations. Before you could say, "Man and wife," he was standing at the altar before Father Adonis or Reverend Sampson, eager to tie the knot with a persevering woman friend whom he had formerly tried to elude.

"Suh whuh she tell you?" my mother asked.

'Gatha put down the tape measure and sat down again at her sewing table. I pretended that I was engrossed in a copy of a *Today's Bride* fashion magazine I had found on the coffee table in the living room. I knew my mother could not very well dismiss me from this conversation and kept my eyes glued to the picture of a white model in a Christian Dior bridal gown who looked out from the pages with a glassy stare.

"Well, when A see dat 'e railly din inten' to do nutt'n after A was pregnant wid dis one, A visit Mama Rose. She tell me to light a candle every time A bathe an' keep it on a shelf in de batchroom."

I tried to guage the probability of a candle's staying lit in a damp bathroom.

"Den she tell me dat when A bathe, A mus' have a blue bath." 'Gatha began to giggle in whispers, her large belly shaking with silent laughter.

"Well you know is right away A had to move to mi *Ricketts Crown*," she said.

"After dat, she seh A mus' *steam* 'e food for a week." Believers in obeah regarded steaming as a woman's infallible course for securing the affections of a reluctant male on whom she had set her sights. 'Gatha rocked with silent laughter, but my mother looked worried.

"But gyurl," my mother said, her brow furrowed, "Whuh gun happen if 'e fine out?"

"How de hell 'e gun fine out?" 'Gatha asked spiritedly. My mother detested Eustace and was on close terms with 'Gatha who was therefore fairly sure that her secret was secure. 'Gatha continued.

"To besize, 'e deserve it. You know how long dat man had me, stringin' me along, an got all 'e woman dem mekkin deh eye pass me? After I get all dese chirren, is time 'e mek me a respectable woman. Afta rall, *goat en bite me*! 'E does come hay an' always want somet'ing fuh eat when 'e en even put a cent in meh han'. De ol' people seh *'kineness mek crappo en got tail,'* an' *dis* crappo (here 'Gatha paused and stuck her forefinger into the middle of her ample chest) bin kine too long."

None of us noticed that Eustace had stopped snoring.

"Gyurl! De food ready yet? You out deh busy *talkin' name,* an' A sure de food en done yet. When you gun fix me up?" he called impatiently from the bedroom.

"Soon darlin', soon," 'Gatha said sweetly, getting up to go to the kitchen.

With a soft, satiny rustle, the unfinished white bridal gown slid from the sewing machine to the floor. A cool north-east breeze touched the fringes of the heat shimmering over the village, and, in the distance, a cock crowed.

CHAPTER 7

On my first day in high school, I wheeled my bike into its curved driveway, my heart beating fearfully. My mother had bought me a new *Raleigh* bicycle, and the thrill of riding it alone all the way to the city was diminished by my fear of the unknown. In spite of the added volume of work that she had had in connection with the wedding, 'Gatha had done a good job with my school uniforms. After my mother had finished combing my hair that she had washed the day before, I inspected my appearance in her bedroom mirror. Everything was in order—the green and red school crest on the band of my Panama hat that was held in place with a length of elastic under my chin, my green and red striped school tie, white shirt, green uniform with leather school purse, the strap of which was slung diagonally across my chest, white socks and black shoes. It occurred to me that, except for my Black physical features, I looked like the pictures of English school girls I had seen in the books of Angela Brazil, the English children's novelist. A picture of the Chief in his riding gear flashed through my mind. I said good-bye to Gwennie Braithwaite who would remain at the village school to take the *school-leaving* examination. As I left Kitty that morning, I felt as though I were leaving it forever.

I arrived at school sweating from the three-mile ride to the city. There were other "new girls" some of whom had come from as far away as Buxton, the historic little East

Coast village that had been bought by freed slaves who had pooled their meagre resources to purchase the old slave plantation from its former colonial owners. Groups of returning students stood around the entrance near the bicycle racks to comment upon, or greet, the new arrivals. They had composure and self-assurance that I had never seen in my fellow village students. I looked around for Drupattie who would be coming from Kitty on the Kitty-Lamaha bus, but it seemed that she had not yet arrived. After I deposited my bicycle in the racks, a prefect escorted a group of us "new girls" to our classrooms.

Here for the first time, I had my own desk and chair. Among the students at the village school, there was always jockeying for space at long desks and benches that we shared. Here, more than with anything else, I was thrilled at having my own writing space. It was like a tiny island over which only I had control, and I revelled in it. I could look out the row of windows past the huge old mango trees on the closely shaven school lawns, right onto Carmichael Street and beyond and simply let my imagination take flight. Just outside the formroom, I also had my own locker where I stored my books and other belongings. Drupattie arrived, and she sat at a desk next to mine. We said little to each other, but we shared a silent closeness in our thoughts of the village from which we had struggled to get to this place. The school bell rang, and we all settled down.

Along with other "new girls," I was placed in the Lower Third. In this form, besides the new entrants, there were other girls who had been admitted the previous year. They were special entrants who were either the daughters of expatriates or of the local professional class, and who had gained entry to the school through an entrance examination and special interview. Unlike the parents of the scholarship winners, their parents paid their tuition. Most of them came from the exclusive elementary convent school in suburban Queenstown, and many of them seemed to hold themselves aloof from the rest of the class, unless they had known some one of us previously.

A young Black woman entered the formroom. The first things that struck me about her were her firm self-assured step and the direct way in which she met our sheepish looks. Her hair was neatly pressed and curled, and she wore a simple but quietly stylish cotton dress. Her eyes swept the formroom as the girls who already knew the school's protocol stood up, and the rest of us scrambled to our feet. She stood there quietly at her desk until all murmurs melted into silence.

"Good morning, girls."

"Good morning, Miss Burgess." "Miss Burgess" was added by the girls who already knew her.

"I am Miss Elaine Burgess. You may all sit, and you may call me Miss Burgess. I shall be your form-mistress this term."

She wrote her name on the blackboard as we sat down again.

I had heard my father mention Elaine Burgess four of five years before when, as he lay reading the *Daily Chronicle* in the Berbice chair in our sitting room, he had remarked to my mother, "Eh, eh gyurl! A notice dat Elaine Burgess get de Guiana dis year." There had been a picture of Elaine Burgess in her white shirt and school tie above an article reporting that she had excelled at the Senior Cambridge examination and had won the Guiana Scholarship. She had gone on to a Scottish university where she had studied British history, Latin, and Greek and, upon graduation, had returned to the colony to teach Latin and British history at her *alma mater*. At that time, no one questioned the dubious relevance of these subjects to the needs of a poverty-stricken colonial territory on the brink of independence. None asked why the scarce resources of the British Guianese tax-payers should have been used in the costly Guiana scholarship for such study. We only knew that Elaine Burgess was a Guianese woman who had outshone all others, and we were proud. She had skipped across the ocean where many of us had never been and crossed her wits with some of the world's intellectual best, graduating with first class honors. She had then returned to the colony to help some of its other daughters do the same.

She read our names from the form register, with each of us replying "Here" when we heard our names. When she came to Drupattie's name, Miss Burgess said, "Tell me your last name."

Drupattie had no last name. Like some other East Indians, she had only one name, a fact that we had all accepted unquestioningly at the village school.

"Drupattie is my only name, Miss," Drupattie said, her eyes on the floor.

There was a snigger from the front rows where the girls who had been admitted the year before had taken up their positions.

"Very well, Drupattie. You may sit," Miss Burgess said, warningly eyeing the source of the sniggers.

Drupattie sat down, a slow blush starting up from her neck and spreading under her olive skin, up across her face.

"As members of this school, you 'new girls' have now entered into a proud tradition. You will be expected to conduct yourselves like young ladies. You are required to wear your hats at all times when you are in school uniform outside of this building. You will be clean and tidy and wear the complete school uniform. No jewelry is allowed—no earrings or bangles."

She said this eyeing Drupattie's gold bangles with slightly raised eyebrows. Drupattie began to slide them off her wrists.

"You will not run in the school corridors, nor will you lean on the railings of the corridors. You will speak quietly and properly at all times. When any other mistress enters this formroom, you will all rise and then sit when you are told to do so. There is to be no eating in the formroom. If these rules are broken you will be punished with detentions and order marks. Is that understood girls?"

We all chorused, "Yes, Miss Burgess."

I would soon learn that these were only a few of the school's rules.

"The school's motto is 'Whatsoever thy hand findeth to do, do it with thy might.' The school expects you to do your best at all times," she concluded.

It was clear from her remarks—from everything that we had everheard about this school—that there would be none of the corporal punishment so prevalent in almost all of the schools from which we "scholarship girls" had come. Yet, I associated the prospect of order marks and detentions with an ignominy that was comparable with the physical pain of Mr. Isaac Davis' "Little Nell."

Many of the other "new girls" had come from elementary schools in Georgetown where the headmasters like Mr. Theophilus Griffith, Mr. Joseph Alphonso, and Mr. Emmanuel Carrington, all liberal users of the cane, had secured a reputation for themselves as groomers of scholarship winners. In essence, the village school was a microcosm of the colonial experience, with the headmaster as the autocratic governor of a little academic colony where severe discipline went unquestioned even by parents. When one spoke of each of these headmasters, it was often with the use of the title, "Mr.," and both his first and last names. For instance, one referred to "Mr. Theophilus Griffith," never simply to "Mr. Griffith."

In earlier years, headmasters were paid according to their scholarship successes—one reason why they themselves often undertook the teaching of the scholarship classes and partly why many of them were so merciless in their use of the cane. Indeed, the quality of education at an elementary school was then measured in terms of the person of the headmaster and his school's scholarship successes.

The result was the marginalization of those students who were unsuccessful in, or ignored by, the scholarship process—students like Gwennie, Joe-Joe, and Winston Braithwaite who were then destined to progress through the village elementary school's school-leaving and *pupilteacher* classes (if they were lucky). Or they would be so demoralized by repeated brutality that they would flee to the "luck-and-chance" existence of survival without skills among the masses of the colony. This educational system also groomed a local professional middle class that sprang from the ranks of "scholarship boys and girls." The leading boys' and girls' secondary schools were an important stage in this grooming process.

It sometimes happened that a pupil not admitted to the scholarship class would successfully take the school-leaving examination at the age of about sixteen. Then he would enter the margins of government service as, for example, a "post boy" or general helper in the post office. If he were ambitious and determined enough, he might be able to save enough for passage to England or the United States and go on to make something of himself professionally. Some girls who passed the pupil-teacher examination might go on to make teaching a career while others like my mother might become nurses. However, for the masses of Guianese women in 1958, legal or common-law marriage remained common escape routes out of penury into ostensible economic and social stability.

The sound of a brass gong reverberated through the corridors, and escorted by two prefects, we filed singly out of the formroom and into the large hall for prayers, along with other students from other form rooms all over the school. Around us on the walls of the hall were large rectangular wooden plaques listing the names of Guianese girls who had brought honor to the school in academics or athletics. Here, dating back to the early twenties, was the list of girls who had been Guiana scholars. Miss Burgess' name was among them. Another list bore the names of girls who had been the school's past games captains. Even in adult years, when I would visit this hall, I still felt encircled by the same quiet, surging sense of female historicity and valorization that I had experienced that first morning in early September, so many years before.

The headmistress and teaching staff walked unto the platform, and we all scrambled to our feet. The headmistress was a little, bespectacled, gray-haired Englishwoman who, in spite of her fiftyish look, still retained a rather athletic figure.

All the other members of the teaching staff were women, some of them white Englishwomen, and others, like Miss Burgess, locally born. The headmistress spoke encouragingly, urging us to do our best that term. She led us in prayer, and then we sang the hymn, "Lord Behold Us With Thy Blessing," followed by the school hymn, "Look Down On Us O Father." Immediately after assembly, we went home and returned the next day for regular classes. Drupattie and I would have marvelled had we been able to stare into the great pregnant belly of the future, and foresee the pain and joy we would feel in this hall as we grew to young womanhood, ringed by female spirits that had gone before us.

CHAPTER 8

I hold in my hand a brown, fading photograph of my mother and father taken in May 1946, a month before I was born. As an adult, I find that I no longer just glance at the photograph and pass on to more interesting things in the way that I used to when I was a child. Increasingly now, I search both faces for some clue of what was happening in their lives and minds at the moment when the photographer at Adams' Photo Studio on Camp Street ordered them with imperious urgency to "Smile!"

My mother told me that it was Sunday afternoon, and the hot cramped front office of the studio was crowded with waiting families and individuals dressed in their Sunday best, the children fresh from three o'clock Sunday Schools in Georgetown—little Black boys wriggling inside uncomfortable, itchy, starched collars of lily white cotton shirts, their legs, shined with *Vaseline* by mothers determined to rub some of the blackness out of them, protruding like sticks from beneath short, warm, dark serge pants, their knotty hair brushed flat into tight disciplined respectability; and little Black girls, their hair tightly plaited and secured with colourful hair ribbons, their scalps gleaming with coconut oil or castor oil in the parts, their crocheted socks sagging down under their heels inside the backs of their shoes, their legs and faces shined—all waiting to have memories of first communion, confirmation, or, in the case of some of the adults, wedding anniversaries and engagements, captured for posterity.

Here is my mother, a young Black woman of twenty-six whose real skin shade, the black and white photograph does not truly reflect. Her large, soft eyes are dull, her back is already slightly bent with the awareness of her future as a wife and mother in a country that had always seemed to be recovering from the colonial ravages of a World War that went well beyond just Hitler and Germany. Her lips are parted softly and very slightly as if she were going to say something to the cameraman, but realizing that it does not matter, she closes them slowly in mild resignation. Her carefully pressed hair is rolled on top and to the sides of her head in two upswept folds in the style of Joan Crawford whom she has seen in *Mildred Pierce* at the Astor Cinema on Church Street. She is wearing a dress of black and white material (the photograph does not permit my imagining more colour), with a fussy kind of white collar with ends that point outward from each shoulder. I cannot miss the protrusion of her lower abdomen for she is in her eighth month of pregnancy. I wonder what she thought of me then as I slept under her heart; if, had she known that I was a girl, she would have been as filled with pride as some men are for their sons; or if she would have feared for my future as a Black woman—a coloured girl in the ring.

And I look at my father in the photograph. He is wearing a double-breasted serge suit, starched cotton shirt and broad striped tie. At twenty-seven, his hairline is already showing signs of receding, and his dark eyes look levelly and self-confidently at the camera from behind horn-rimmed glasses. He holds himself with the soldier's erectness, and his arm is wrapped protectively around my mother's shoulders with a clear self-consciousness of her pregnancy. He is home on leave from Barbados where he has been stationed for some months as a sergeant in the British Royal Army Medical Corps, a fact that he regards with a great deal of pride. Even though the war is over, he has not yet been demobilized from the army and has just gotten off a ship a few days ago on short special leave, granted after much bureacratic manoeuvring, so that he may come home in time to marry my mother before my birth. I look at his eyes and see the hope for a son, a man-child who will do manly, military things that make countries proud. Soon after this photograph is taken, he and my mother will be married, and he will be back in uniform and will return to Barbados before being demobilized in another few months.

I returned home from my first day at school, eager to tell my parents about my experience. My mother listened quietly, but her eyes had the same dull look I had seen in the photograph. My father had come home unexpectedly early, and he sat quietly in the Berbice chair. I knew that something was wrong.

"What is it, Mama?" I asked.

She did not answer but turned away to the bedroom to start getting ready for the two to ten shift at the Public Hospital.

"I've been transferred to Apaiqua," my father answered. "I'm going to be the Government Dispenser there." For him, serious matters like these required the use of Standard English.

Apaiqua was hundreds of miles away in the Mazaruni, far into the almost inaccessible interior of the country, approachable only by a small British Guiana Airways 'amphibious' plane. It landed in the Mazaruni river, from which a small launch took passengers to the little settlement that was virtually a tiny clearing in the forest. For a moment, I thought anxiously only of myself, wondering if this new development meant that I would have to leave my new school and go to live there.

"I will go to work there," my father continued quietly. "And your mother will stay here with you and Bernard to see to your schooling while I am away. I'll come back to see you all from time to time. And I won't be there forever. Most dispensers get transferred out of town from time to time."

I had never felt very close to my father and had never been able to dispel the feeling that he was disappointed when his first child turned out to be a girl. He had chosen a boy's name when he had heard that my mother was pregnant, but when I turned up in the delivery room, he had left my naming to my mother and Grammudduh. He had always appeared to me to be stern, sometimes aloof, often remote, retreating behind reading material where he could scarcely be reached. Yet, it was he who taught me to read when, as a young child, I peered over his shoulder at the *Daily Chronicle*. Then, hearing his rare chuckle as he read the comic strips, I would ask him to explain what he was reading, and he would point out the words in the balloons over the characters' heads. He was an avid reader who devoured the literary classics, then, as I grew older, passed them over to me. By the time that I was twelve, in addition to various "penny-dreadfuls," and *True Romance* magazines that I was careful to read away from his notice, I had become familiar with the lives of literature's great orphans in books like *Oliver Twist, Great Expectations and David Copperfield*. Still, for me, my father generally remained as inaccessible as the Mazaruni to which he was now going. The thought of his imminent departure left me with the sad realization that, never really having felt emotionally close to him, I would now lose even his physical presence.

My mother loved him with almost the same passion she had felt that Sunday afternoon twelve years before in Adams' Photo Studio, and she took his departure rather badly. The night before he left, after Bernard and I were in bed, they sat in the *Demerara* moonlight over the little platform at the top of our front steps, as they had done so many times before, their voices unusually low, listening to music broadcast from the BBC in London. From the *Phillips* radio in our living room, came the sounds of Victor Sylvester's orchestra playing "Till The End of Time" and then "The White Cliffs of Dover," two of their special songs during their long wartime separation.

The next morning, before Bernard and I left for school, a little white *Morris Minor* Booker's taxi stopped at our gate, and my parents got into it to make the trip to the British Guiana Airways Terminal from where my mother saw my father off. Bernard and I stood at the gate waving them goodbye. As the taxi turned the corner taking them away from Lamaha Street, I had the curious, sinking feeling that I had lost them both and that our family would never again be the same.

CHAPTER 9

One Saturday morning some weeks later, as I went to Miss Edna's to buy black pudding, I passed a blue *Vauxhall* car parked a few doors down from her gate. I took little notice of the well-groomed Black woman of about forty, dressed in green, who sat behind the steering wheel. When I got to Miss Edna's, her niece, Shirley, was sitting in the living room. Shirley was sprawled in a Morris chair, her legs outspread, her head thrown back, one arm extended languidly over the arm of the chair, a lit *Lighthouse* cigarette held between her index and middle fingers. She was small, attractive and shapely, with thick luxuriant black hair that her early hairdressing experience had enabled her to groom to perfection. Now, however, with her hair awry, she looked sick and listless as she snapped the fingers of her free hand to the sounds of "Doggie in the Window" emanating from the gramophone. Her large eyes stared vacantly at some looming grief, visible only to her. Occasionally, she would squirm as though she were sore.

Miss Edna, Miss Ada and Miss Ida were in the kitchen going about their usual Saturday business of making black pudding and other delicacies for sale. Now and then, the women would peek in at Shirley and speak in low whispers to make sure that she did not hear them above the sound of the gramophone. As I waited in the kitchen for the black pudding, Miss Ada said, "It look like she comin' rung. O Lord, T'ursday night she was feelin' too bad.

At leas' de bleedin stop, an' she could drink de lil ochroe soup A give 'er to keep she strengt' up."

"Yes, chile," Miss Edna replied. "In anodda few days she should be much better."

Her bloodied hands worked feverishly, stuffing the cow's blood and rice through the funnel into the cow's intestines. Now and then she passed the back of her hand across her forehead, leaving a streak of blood that made her look like she had a head wound. The kitchen reeked with the smell of cow's blood and married man pork, the black pudding herb.

"De Lord will punish boat uh y'all fuh aidin' an abettin' sin," Miss Ida chimed in sanctimoniously. "Ada an' Edna, why y'all encourage Shirley to *tek she belly an' mek it buryin' grung,* only God know. To besize, dis midwife dat she go to, don' know what de hell she doin'. (Here Miss Ida abandoned her usual scrupulous avoidance of expletives since I suppose she felt that the gravity of the situation warranted such a lapse). Only two years ago, Dolores John dat livin' up by de seawall get lockjaw after dis same midwife try help she fuh t'row 'way she baby. Is only a miracle de save poe Dolores. To dis day, Dolores still *kyan* get pregnant again. Y'all try. Dere will be weepin' an' wailin' an gnashin' of teet'. A tellin' alyou." She emphasized this last bit wagging her long, bony finger.

Miss Edna was not in the least bit perturbed by these dire predictions.

"Look Ida," she said in a spirited whisper, turning around and sprinkling blood from the funnel on the kitchen floor as she did so. "Shirley mek she decision an' she mus' know what she want. A was well prepared to help mine de pickney even dough Shirley rightly point out dat it woulda been hard. If de manager at de Blue Lantern de fine out she de get chile for a customer, he might a de fire she."

Miss Ada, who had listened quietly to these exchanges,

then added, "Yes, an' den wheh we woulda been? Wheh we woulda been, Ida? A ask you! I already strugglin' wid two odda chirren in dis lil halfa house. We already nearly out pun de road as it is. A suppose you an yuh Jesus would a help we when we had one mo' pickney mout to feed!"

"O ye blasphemers! O ye of little fait'!" Miss Ida said in a loud whisper. "Alyou countenance Shirley in one sin suh she could continue in anodda. 'Lord how long shall de wicked triumph?'" she asked, quoting from the Book of Psalms.

Whenever Miss Ida felt herself cornered by reality, she would quickly resort to some appropriate Biblical quotation. At this point, the women were interrupted by Shirley's stiff entry into the kitchen. It was clear that the backstreet abortion had left her considerably weakened and sore. She wreaked faintly of cigarette smoke and looked thinner than when I had last seen her. The in-vogue "hobble" skirt that she then wore and which had previously been tight-fitting, now hung loosely around her hips and thighs.

"A t'ink a will go *dung tung* an' see if Jimmy got mi money," she said in a low, dead voice. Jimmy was the manager of the Blue Lantern, and he paid his employees on Saturday mornings.

"Why you don' wait till you feelin' better?" Miss Ada asked.

"Sometimes is hard to fine Jimmy if you don' ketch 'e pun a Saturday mornin'," Shirley answered. "A gun tek de Kitty-Lemaha bus an' come back quick-quick."

Miss Ada opened her mouth to protest, but Shirley walked through the sitting room and out the front door of the cottage. For several minutes, the women continued with their conversation—Miss Ida's Biblical injunctions interspersed with Miss Ada's and Miss Edna's justifications. The flies buzzed, the Virgin Mary continued to look complacently from the diocesan calendar, and a mild breeze ruffled the leaves of the sappodila tree in the backyard.

Suddenly we heard screams from the road that ran in front of the house.

"Miss Edna come quick! Come quick! Come quick-quick! A lady beatin' de hell outa Shirley out hey! Is Miss Cromwell!"

This was the voice of Mildred, Shirley's friend who lived next door and who had put Shirley in touch with the midwife. We all rushed to the front door, and for a brief moment there was jostling as Miss Ada and Miss Edna tried to squeeze their bulky bodies through the narrow doorway at the same time. On the road, the woman I had passed sitting in the parked blue *Vauxhall* had Shirley by the hair with one hand and, with the other, was pummelling her in the abdomen. A crowd was gathering fast to observe the incident, and some idle youths, whose attentions Shirley had spurned in the past, urged Mrs. Cromwell on.

"Yuh dirty little bitch!" Mrs. Cromwell cried. "Leave mi husban' alone! Yuh gettin' baby fuh he? I gun cuff it out uh yuh, yuh lil whore!"

Mrs. Cromwell was a well-built woman, taller, stronger and sturdier than Shirley. In any event, Shirley's weakened condition made the encounter even more unequal. Mrs. Cromwell now bore no resemblance to the chic woman in green whom I had seen sitting so sedately in her car earlier. She was like a bull that a sadistic matador had driven insane. Apparently she was well aware that Shirley made a regular Saturday morning trip to the city for her pay, and, daunted by the support she knew Shirley would have received from her friends in the tough Tiger Bay area of the Blue Lantern, Mrs. Cromwell had decided to attack her where she was most vulnerable and where she and her relatives would feel the most shame—in the neighborhood where they lived.

"Who de hell she t'ink she is," squeaked Mildred, referring to Mrs. Cromwell.

"*She?* Who de rass you callin' '*she?*' *She is de kyat's mudduh; he is de four-footed fadduh,*" cried Mrs. Cromwell, pausing in her attack on Shirley and turning threateningly around to Mildred.

Before Miss Edna and her sisters could get past the gate, Mrs. Cromwell had given Shirley a violent parting shove, kicked off her own *Baby Doll* shoes, and run to her car. She took off with a loud roar of the engine in a cloud of dust, the car shrilling in first gear and nearly running over the idle, young male onlookers who had gathered to amuse themselves and who jumped out of the car's path in the nick of time.

Battered, bleeding, and crying, Shirley collapsed on the dusty roadside. Miss Edna and her sisters all tried to lift her to her feet, gently bearing her weight as they took her indoors past the tittering spectators.

"M'dear dat is what yuh does get when yuh guh lookin' fuh *whuh yuh en put dung,*" said Auntie Joycie, a woman who had a cakeshop across the street from Miss Edna's house and who was in direct competition with her for the neighborhood business.

"Is true! True-true! True-true! Dese young gyurls like deh kyan keep deh hands to dehself." This from Miss Mavis, Auntie Joycie's cousin and general helper in the cakeshop.

For the first time, I saw Miss Edna speechless. She kept repeating, " Eh eh! Eh eh! Well look 'pon my *crosses*! Some people could be *suh* pre*sum*ptious! Well look at my crosses!" as she and Miss Ada manoeuvered Shirley towards the house.

Miss Ida seemed to feel an uneasy satisfaction that her predictions about Shirley's lifestyle were borne out. She quoted again from the Book of Psalms: "When de wicked spring as de grass, and when all de workers of iniquity do

71

flourish; it is dat dey shall be destroyed forever." Miss Edna suddenly recovered herself and turned upon Miss Ida with the near hiss of a *labaria*: "Ida! Shut yuh blasted mout' an' go an' gedde police!"

An hour later, Police Constable Eustace King sat in Miss Edna's living room, Mrs. Cromwell's discarded *Baby Doll* shoes on the floor near his feet, a plate of steaming black pudding in his lap. From the radio next door came the sounds of The Mighty Sparrow, the young Trinidadian calypsonian, singing "Jean and Dinah." As Eustace interrogated the hapless Shirley, his hot eyes devoured her body under the tight, red, seersucker blouse. Once, briefly, he paused in his investigative work and looked up at the living room wall to the picture of Jesus with His arms outstretched from His bleeding heart. He met Eustace's gaze with a cold, blue-eyed indifference.

CHAPTER 10

No one could have foretold where this sequence of events involving Eustace, Shirley and Mrs. Cromwell would lead, and had we villagers been able to, we would surely have been awed by the creaking wheel of fate that could knock us off the edge of life's muddy road and then grind ineluctably on. Suffice it to say that when Eustace met Shirley, he became enamoured of her to the exclusion of everyone else. In the ensuing days, he was a frequent visitor to Miss Edna's, carrying out what he officiously termed "follow-up investigative procedures," and, more in the service of his own motives than for any official reasons, questioning Shirley intensively and intrusively about her relationship with James Cromwell.

Soon, like a faintly disguised suitor, he came bearing gifts—the odd large-sized *Cadbury's* chocolate bar; or the bottle of *Evening in Paris* perfume that he just happened to see in Tang's drug store when he was in Georgetown that day; or, to keep Miss Ada's good will, a jar of *Vicks Vaporub* for her lumbago. He seemed to have forgotten his impending marriage, and later on, according to Miss Edna, when Shirley reminded him of it, he said of 'Gatha, "Oh she? I only promise to marry she suh she could ring off uh me an' stop runnin' me into court. De woman t'ink dat she gun hook me wid baby, but she got anodda t'ink comin'." Shirley, for her part, remained distant but not aloof, leaving just enough of a crack in the door of her reserve to maintain his interest.

I cannot tell you what was passing through Shirley's mind and heart when she heard Eustace's callous dismissal and indictment of 'Gatha, whether or not she had felt a hurt woman's empathy with another bleeding sister. Reflecting on it now from a woman's perspective, I can only surmise that the hard knocks that poverty and Mrs. Cromwell had dealt Shirley had congealed in her young bleeding heart, leaving her calculating, hurt and hard. Before Mrs. Cromwell's humiliating assault, Shirley had taught me the new calypso dance called the "zeg" that was then the craze. As her gramophone blared the words, "Zeg! Zeg! Zeg! Mama, zeg if you zegging," she gyrated in the little sitting room, encouraging me to do the dance moves with her, and yelling, "Come on gyurl, zeg!" She also told me secret woman-things about men and the facts of life in earthy phrases that would have angered mother had she known. Yet Shirley opened up for me an important window, a kind of initiation into womanhood in our culture, one that I would not have gotten from textbooks or from the socially restrictive atmosphere of the secondary school. Time would reveal how much more I was yet to learn from the choices she made in her life.

Thirty years later, from her sick-bed in the Alms House, the retirement home for the aged poor on Brickdam, Miss Edna told me that soon after his initial interrogation of Shirley, Eustace went to James Cromwell's office. Eustace confronted Cromwell with his wife's assault on Shirley, and showing him the discarded *Baby Doll* shoes, Eustace made Cromwell an offer: In return for Eustace's successfully persuading Shirley to drop the case against his wife, Cromwell would end the relationship with Shirley. In Miss Edna's view, while Cromwell was greatly infatuated with Shirley, the occasion of her pregnancy and subsequent abortion caused him some trepidation. He was less concerned for Shirley's physical safety than fearful of the public discovery of his own complicity. Also, Shirley had become increasingly demanding in the course of their relationship even as his wife had grown more shrewish with her knowledge of the affair.

Furthermore, his wife's dogging Shirley's heels in the area of the Blue Lantern carried with it scandalous possibilities that Cromwell shuddered to contemplate. He lived in fear of his wife's wrath and her absolute willingness to carry out every threat she made. Cromwell was proud of his position in the Civil Service; his two children were at the leading boys' secondary school, and he and his wife were well-respected members of St. Andrew's Church in Georgetown. The Blue Lantern was part of the hidden, seedier, darker side of his nature, and he wanted it to remain so. He was also seriously being considered for promotion to Principal Assistant Secretary in the government department where he worked, and a court case with his wife as a defendant charged with assaulting his paramour would surely spell the end of his hopes for professional advancement. I can imagine that when Eustace approached him, Cromwell was haunted by the nightmarish possibility of Shirley, Mrs. Cromwell and himself being featured in the humorous "Around The Courts" column of the *Daily Chronicle* if the matter went to court. He eagerly agreed to Eustace's proposal.

It was Saturday night—a few days before 'Gatha's wedding—and her relatives and friends were assembled in her lamplit backyard over which hung the full moon. It was the night of the *queh-queh* when we would all sing folk songs and play ring games, some of the festivities associated with the impending wedding. Under the tamarind tree in the backyard, groups of men played dominoes and drank rum from little snap glasses. Clapping rhythmically as they sang the folksong, "Missie Los' She Gol' Ring," women and girls formed a circle around 'Gatha who moved from person to person inside the circle looking for the "gold ring." Now and then, the men under the tamarind tree would join in the chorus, their baritone and tenor voices ringing out a descant:

Fine am, fine am, fine am, fine aaaaamm—
Fine am an' leh me see.

Auntie Joycie sat on the back steps with the younger children telling them "'nancy stories" and "ole time stories." Neighbors and friends had brought mince patties, cook-up rice, chow mein and other delicacies. Miss Edna had sent black pudding, but neither she nor her sisters had come, possibly because of their guilty feeling of involvement in Eustace's attentions to Shirley who was also absent from the queh-queh festivities. As the women started to sing the folk song, "Satira Gal," the elderly Miss Mavis got into the ring, raising her skirt to thigh level, and swivelling her hips to the chorus: "Oh Sityra, mo' man deh, Oh Sityra mo' man deh." Her gyrations increased the general tempo and temperature of the celebration. This was the same Miss Mavis who had supported Auntie Joycie's deprecation of Shirley after Mrs. Cromwell's attack.

'Gatha broke away from the ring and came over to remark anxiously to my mother that she had not seen Eustace in the last two days. He had promised to be there for the queh-queh but added that he might be late because he was deeply involved in the ongoing investigation of an important case.

I had seen him at Miss Edna's that morning. With a rumpled appearance, he emerged from the little back room where Shirley usually slept and was soon followed by an equally dishevelled Shirley, who told me that her mother and aunts had not yet returned from the slaughterhouse and market where they had gone to get the ingredients for their day's work. My mother had strict rules about my minding my own business.

"You mus' see but don' talk!" she would say. "See but don' talk! *Don' put yuh mout' in big people business!*" I therefore listened quietly to the anxiety, doubt and pain that crept into 'Gatha's tone and watched with her for Eustace's arrival. He never came.

The next day, in tears, 'Gatha visited my mother, her unfinished wedding dress in a bag. Having just returned from church, my mother had changed out of her "good things" and was beginning to get her pot of the usual Sunday split pea soup going. When she saw 'Gatha's agitation, she left me to stir the pot and went into the sitting room to talk to her. From the kitchen, I could hear 'Gatha clearly, her voice rising in anguish. It seemed that Eustace had come home early that morning, told her the wedding was off, gathered together his belongings, and left for good. For her part, 'Gatha had been prepared to light angrily into him when he finally came home, but this surprising new development left her defensively apologetic, pleading and hysterical. He had ignored 'Gatha's entreaties for an explanation or discussion of what had led to his decision. In the past, even when she had taken him to court, Eustace had never attempted to leave her. He had often threatened to do so, but he and 'Gatha had seemed to have some sort of silent agreement yoking them together in their misery. It was an arrangement that, in time, everyone else took for granted and to which everyone else, by doing so, was party, so that my mother was now as surprised as 'Gatha.

"Auntie Joycie di' hint to me dat 'e was seein' Shirley, but A din believe," 'Gatha sobbed. "You know how Auntie Joycie could be *fas'* an' malicious when she get ready."

My mother made no reply to this. When we were out of her presence, Auntie Joycie, like Miss Ida, was one of my mother's eyes and ears for Bernard's behaviour and mine. 'Gatha had removed the bridal gown from the bag and, as she sobbed, clutched it to her, almost as though she were seeking from it some sort of protection against the grief that now descended on her.

Moved by 'Gatha's tears, my mother had begun to cry.

"Doan worry gyurl," she sniffed, wiping her own tears and 'Gatha's with the hand-embroidered handkerchief that she always kept in her dress pocket. "Dat wretch gun get what 'e deserve. You mark my words! 'E gun get what 'e deserve. You jus' look to yuh God, yuh chirren an' yuhself."

But it was a long time before 'Gatha was able to heed this advice. Stung by the humiliation of having been jilted, she remained indoors, crying endlessly, her life-saving sewing machine gathering dust in a corner of the sitting room. When neighbors and friends did not take care of them, her children went neglected, and she herself ate little, seeming to forget the young life she carried. Just as we were beginning to think that she was losing her mind, her relatives finally intervened temporarily to take care of her and her children. Some months later, 'Gatha was delivered of a stillborn infant daughter. The life-and-death-dealing umbilical cord tightly encircled her little neck. Her tiny body was so anemic and undersized that even had she lived, she would have had little chance in the world from which she was so early taken.

One Saturday morning a few weeks later, Miss Ada stood in the kitchen in the midst of black pudding preparations reading a letter that Burchell, the postman, had just delivered. Burchell's arrival had caught Miss Ida in loud mid-hum of the hymn, "Bringing In The Sheaves." Up to her wrists in flour, Miss Edna stood rolling out the dough for patties and pine-tarts. Beads of sweat were already beginning to form on her brow as the tropical ten o'clock heat began a kind of slow, silent, skillet-like sizzle. For a few moments after she had torn open the envelope, Miss Ada read the letter, her lips slowly forming the words, her bloody fingers trembling slightly. She moved unsteadily over to a rickety bench in the kitchen and sat down, the letter in her hand that was now resting on her lap. A fly lighted on the letter, crawled over the dried blood on her hand and then flew off, settling on the calendar Virgin's smug smile.

"Wha' happen to you, Ada? Who write you? Is bad news? Wha' happen gyurl?" asked Miss Ida for whom the contents of personal letters were matters to be shared, regardless of their nature.

"Why you suh fas', Ida?" asked Miss Edna, even as she herself edged closer to Miss Ada and craned her neck to get a look at the letter's contents. "Is Eustace," replied Miss Ada. "'E write home fuh Shirley."

A male suitor would "write home" to the head of the family asking permission to marry the daughter or ward of the household. The custom was taken very seriously by many Guianese families, especially those of the Black middle class, who saw it as an indication of a male suitor's serious interest in, and respect for, the object of his affection. Indeed, many a male suitor who had sat in a young woman's parlor whispering sweet nothings to her on too many occasions over too long a period without "writing home" stood a good chance of being sternly approached by the head of the household. He would then be asked to give a clear account of his intentions with regard to the young woman in question and to *address the house properly.*

Shirley's occupation at the Blue Lantern put her outside the pale of social acceptability associated with a respectable young woman for whom a man would "write home." Moreover, she had been a participant in an extramarital relationship that had culminated in a shameful public encounter with her lover's wife. Significantly too, while Shirley had not repulsed Eustace's advances, it was never clear that she had ended the relationship with Cromwell once and for all. Some Kitty gossips had reported seeing her and Cromwell one night furtively entering a hotel at Bel Air on the East Coast of Demerara, but this information could not be substantiated. Eustace knew of Shirley's background and was suspicious of her behaviour behind his back. Yet, for all his violent, simmering jealousy, he was still prepared to marry her. Miss Ada recalled that he had summed up his feelings for Shirley to his friend Burchell the postman, saying, "Ah really got *typee* fuh dis woman, yuh know."

I suspect that Eustace's fascination with Shirley lay in the fact that she was probably the first woman to whom he was attracted who was not in awe of him, who showed no shame, regret, fear or guilt regarding her life's circumstances and choices. I also think that, on his part, theirs was still an uncomfortable association. Shirley, after all, was not 'Gatha. He told Burchell that he was certain that marriage would settle her.

In the distance, the voice of old Joe Carter, the village crier, could be heard trailing off as he pedaled his way through the village, ringing his bell and announcing the death of one of the villagers: "Fineral dis afternoon at half-pas' four..." Uneasily, Miss Ada shifted her bulky hips on the little shaky bench that creaked protestingly.

"Y'all might as well hear de letter," she sighed.

"Go on, gyurl. Read it," urged Miss Ida.

" 'Dear Miss Ada,

Hoping the reaches of this my letter finds you basking in the sunshine of good health and God's love as it leaves me the same in His name. I have come to know your daughter Shirley over some time now and find that I am in love with her, believing her to be in love with me. I am therefore asking for your permission to take her hand in marriage and request your blessing in God's name.

Yours in the Lord Eustace Fitzherman King.' "

"Eh Eh! Well Ah tell yuh," preened Miss Ida. "At leas'

de man seem to be a chile uh de Lord, God-fearin' an' all dat. Is good fuh Shirley to get somebody who is righteous t'inkin' in she life suh she can leave dat den of iniquity dat she callin' wuk."

"A chile uh de Lord me foot, Ida!" snarled Miss Edna, sucking her teeth loudly and turning back to her pastry-making. "You yuhself should know dat not everyone dat cry, 'Lord, Lord' is righteous. Doan forget dat dis man is a beatin' sensation when it come to woman. I still don' feel nice 'bout whuh 'e do 'Gatha. Who seh if push come to shove, 'e en gun do de same t'ing to Shirley? In any case, I don' see why Shirley got fuh run an' marry *any cow an' bull foot* jus' because 'e as' she. She young yet; she still got time."

Miss Ada looked doubtful.

"I don' know Edna. You remember when A was young, a fella name Claude Lynch di' 'write home' fuh me, an' you an' Ma read 'e letter an' laugh an' say A could do better? Y'all say dat Claude was jus' a lil post-boy widdout even a *posy* to pee in. I too t'ought dat better would come, suh I refuse Claude even dough A really di' like 'e, an' yuh see how I en' up livin' in a breakin' dung cottage pun de Courentyne wid Reggie who never even put a ring pun me finger? Well Claude was de only person who ever as' me. I never tell yuh dis because A was too shame: But de other day outside Weitin' an' Richter, A run into Claude Lynch. 'E was home on holiday from de States, an' gyurl, 'e look *too* sharp. 'E got a strong yankee accent now, an' 'e say 'e is a big businessman in Brooklyn wid nice wife an' family an' everyt'ing. Ah know 'e was lookin' at me in me one good dress wid de fray out collar an' feelin' sorry fuh me. Edna, A feel *shame suh till!* I don' want dat to happen to Shirley. Life hard enough fuh she as it is, an' knowin' how dese men hay lookin' fuh virgins to marry, Eustace may be de only one to as' she. To besize, 'e got a steady, respectable job, an' if 'e marry she, she will become Mrs. King an' dem like Joycie will never be able to *wash deh mout' pun* she again."

Two weeks later, Eustace rented a cottage near the train line just down the road from Miss Edna. Shirley moved in with him but made no promise to marry him. The routine of daily living continued for Miss Edna, Miss Ada and Miss Ida.

Eventually, 'Gatha overcame the trauma of her child's death and of Eustace's desertion. She buried herself in work, solely supporting herself and her children. Her sewing machine hummed late into the night as she struggled to meet sewing deadlines for brides' dresses and children's school uniforms. Even though Eustace did not support his children or even attempt to see them, she never took him to court again, nor did she ever even mention his name afterward—at least never in my hearing. It was not as if he had died, just never existed. On the rare occasions when their paths crossed in the village, she would move to the other side of the street, staring right through him before she did so, as though he were part of the hot, shimmering air that hovered punishingly over the village.

CHAPTER 11

Secondary school increasingly claimed more of my attention. New subjects like science, French and Latin required my concentration as academic competition between students became intense. Drupattie and I settled into the school routine, and, gradually, we put the incidents taking place in the village on the back burners of our consciousness. Near the end of our first year, Drupattie cut and styled her long hair so that she looked more like the other East Indian girls who attended the secondary school. Many were the daughters of prosperous business or professional people in the city. Some had adopted sophisticated urban attitudes and interests, so Drupattie never mentioned to them the occupation of her father, Ragunandan, who owned a small cakeshop in Kitty, or that of her uncle, Balgobin, who delivered milk.

The front lawns of the school were edged with huge, old mango trees, and during the mango season, we girls who sat near the windows would occasionally raise our eyes from Latin verbs, from Portia's speech in *The Merchant of Venice* or from the adventures of Monsieur Robert in Paris to check to see when ripe mangoes would fall. As soon as the bell rang for the break period, those of us who had noted their location would go tearing across the lawn to get them. Sometimes, some girls who had had their eyes on particularly luscious-looking specimens that still clung tenaciously to the branches would throw bits of wood or bricks up at them in an effort to dislodge them. Such behaviour was against school rules, and if a girl were caught, she would incur the wrath of a teacher or prefect and be thrown into detention.

I still remember some of my high school teachers with affection. One of them was Miss Claywell, an English-woman of about thirty-five. Unmarried, she lived alone in a large house near the Atlantic in the suburb of Kingston. Some years before, she had come out to the colony from Yorkshire to teach English. Everything in her demeanor indicated that she bore her single state with all the exhila-ration that her spirited nature demanded. She sought ev-ery opportunity to go on trips into the interior of the coun-try and revelled in visits to the majestic Kaiteur Fall in the forested, mountainous hinterland, when some of us students had never even crossed the Demerara river. She demon-strated an intense curiosity about the linguistic characteris-tics of Creolese and a serious interest in the poetry of ca-lypso and the musicality of the steel band, forms of creative expression then frowned on as vulgar by many of the local middle class. I made friends among my classmates and started riding to school with Belinda Harrison who lived in Subryanville, the location of my earlier encounter with Justice Day. Eventually, Miss Claywell passed on to Drupattie, Belinda and me the uncritical receptiveness to discovery of our culture that she herself had. Among ourselves, we girls would conjecture about whether or not she had ever had an intimate relationship with a man, for she was still quite at-tractive. In our pubescent imagination, we tried to picture her, panting passionately like Viviene Leigh, locked in the muscular arms of some square-jawed, cleft-chinned Lawrence Olivier-type white colonial administrator. Yet, there was nothing in the scant information that we had about her personal life or in her attitude to indicate that she had this kind of relationship—or that she even pined for it.

In class, she would encourage us to write short stories, and, often in these assignments, I would devote my fancy to stories of English schoolgirls who inevitably trudged long distances over the moors in deep snow to get to school. Or I would write about some young English girl who had undertaken the task of solving some dark mystery connected with an old English abbey or English manor. This was during my Angela-Brazil-and-Enid-Blyton period, when I was immersed in the stories of these two English authors of children's stories. One day, after reading one of my stories, she called me to her desk at the end of the class.

"I like your writing," she said pleasantly. "Have you ever been to England?"

"N-n-n-o," I stammered, pleased by the compliment, but puzzled by the question. Going to England had never seemed within my realm of possibilities.

"Then, don't you think you may write even better about what you know intimately?"

"Like what?" I asked.

"Ooh, I don't know," she replied in that English way she had, propping her chin on the heel of her palm.

It occurred to me then that she was one of the few expatriates I had encountered who did not remind me of the hard, molded, alabaster dolls in Fogarty's show window.

"What about your personal experiences here in this fascinating country?"

Before this, I had never heard the term "fascinating" applied to our local experience. Among the people I knew, life was either a hard, constant struggle to survive on what we often ruefully called "de *mudflat*" or inspiration for hope of escape to England or America. As far as I was concerned, there was nothing "fascinating" about that.

"You know, the time is coming when British Guiana will soon be an independent country. There will be an increasing need for Guianese to record their experiences and their history, to validate their nationhood. Don't *ever* feel that what you have here is unworthy—even if you sense that feeling in the attitudes of some of the adults around you. You give validity to your experience when you write about it. You say to the world, 'Look! We are here, and we are not going away. We have interesting stories to tell—stories that may be different from yours, but no less worthy of being heard.' Enid Blighton has already written her story. Now, you tell yours."

About a month after this exchange, Miss Claywell left British Guiana, and I never saw her again. One morning during school assembly, the headmistress announced that Miss Claywell was returning to England with Mr. Roger Martin, the biology master at the leading secondary school for boys. They had become engaged and would be married in England within a month. It seemed that Viviene Leigh had found Lawrence Olivier.

CHAPTER 12

Coming from an orthodox Hindu background, but living in a Westernized culture, Drupattie's father,
Ragunandan, prided himself on his progressive approach
to matters relating to his own and his family's welfare. He
had initially been disappointed that his wife, Rookmin, had
not given birth to the sons for whom he had longed. He
had had visions of these sons helping him to expand and
improve his little cakeshop and grocery business, or later,
going on to become professional people like the family of
the incumbent Indo-Guianese premier whose progressive
views had so frightened and angered the British government in 1953. However, Ragunandan was delighted when
Drupattie, his daughter and only child, began to show early
signs of academic promise. At the high school we attended,
Drupattie was excelling in biology and other sciences, and
Ragunandan entertained the hope that she would go to the
University of the West Indies in Jamaica, to England, or to
America and study medicine.

"Afta rall," he told my mother, smoke from his *Lighthouse* cigarette funelling out in long billows through his
nostrils, "Times changin' an' gyurl-chirren en only mek fuh
get pickney."

Therefore, while many other young East Indian girls in
the village were being groomed for early wifehood and
motherhood, Ragunandan allowed Drupattie to participate
fully in many of the activities that the less tradition-bound

East Indian parents permitted. On the other hand, Ragunandan's brother and the village milkman, Balgobin, was opposed to such "slackness," as he called it. Balgobin's daughters, Chandrowtie and Lilowtie, were married according to Hindu custom at the ages of thirteen and fourteen, respectively. For them, there would be none of the foolish wastefulness of education. Balgobin married them off to Hindu men with whose parents he made matrimonial arrangements when the two girls were literally still in their cradles. The girls had no say in these choices, but, like good Hindu women, they acquiesced and married these men, who were some years older than they, men whom they had not even seen until the day of the wedding.

Chandrowtie was tied for better or for worse to Lochand who worked as a labourer at the Wales sugar estate on the West Bank of the Demerara River. He drank white rum and beat her habitually while she struggled to raise six children in a small dilapidated *logie* near the sugar estate. Lilowtie fared somewhat better. She was married to Ragubir whose family owned a small sawmilling business on the Courentyne. However, when the first year of their marriage passed and Lilowtie had not conceived, Ragubir, at his family's insistence, reluctantly sent her back to Balgobin even though he (Ragubir) had grown fond of her. Though he did not say it openly, Balgobin blamed Lilowtie solely for her inability to conceive, and just as he was beginning to raise the tempo of his spiteful insinuations, Lilowtie discovered, in the first week after her return home to him, that she was pregnant. Much to Balgobin's relief, she then went back to Ragubir on the Courentyne and disappeared into domesticity.

According to Drupattie, Balgobin was appalled to discover that his brother, Ragunandan, intended to let her remain in high school until her graduation. Why waste time and money educating a girl? Balgobin had asked

Ragunandan as Balgobin sat in the cakeshop drinking from a cold bottle of *Icee Tonic* that, like himself, seemed to sweat from the heat. By the time Drupattie left high school, Balgobin insisted, she would be too old for marriage! What kind of life, he asked, was there for an unmarried, educated East Indian woman? Which East Indian man would want Drupattie if she later became a doctor? It would be madness to send a young girl alone across the ocean into an uncertain and threatening world without a man's protection. That is, *if* she ever managed to become a doctor, given the cost of such an education anyway. An' afta rall, is man who should be docta. Man have fuh feed 'e family. Woman mus' stay home an' mine baby.

With an old folded copy of *Time* magazine, Ragunandan slapped a fly crawling eagerly towards the upturned mauby glasses behind his shop counter and looked levelly at his brother. In spite of his own limited education, Ragunandan had read widely enough to make himself aware of social conditions existing well beyond the boundaries of Hindu culture. Since leaving primary school, he had maintained a pen pal relationship with someone in Connecticut who regularly sent him American news magazines, publications such as the *Reader's Digest* and American newspapers. He was also a devoted listener to the BBC and an ardent reader of the Guianese novelist, Edgar Mittelholzer. Since Ragunandan was earlier diagnosed with diabetes, tiredness had increasingly confined him to the shop where he would read voraciously during the mid-afternoon *sun-hot*.

"Man, wake up!" he cried impatiently to his brother. "Dis is 1960. Times changin', an' we got to change wid dem. A whole worl' out dere across dat ocean dat we don' even know 'bout. All kine uh space exploration goin' on wid Russia and America. One day, deh seh man may even go to de moon. Why den a Eas' Indian woman kyan' be docta an' still get married? Eas' Indian woman is people to."

Balgobin looked momentarily like he was finding it difficult to draw the connection between space exploration and East Indian female experience. Increasingly, of late, he felt that Ragunandan's illness was affecting his good judgement. Drupattie was associating closely with Black girls and with other East Indian girls who routinely cut and styled their hair, encouraged her to do the same, and sat around Booker's snack bar after school talking to young men from the boys' high schools, girls who called Drupattie "Drew!" There was, in this word, a ring of Anglicization that sent an apprehensive shudder through Balgobin's orthodox Hindu sensitivites. In the end, unable to convince his brother that he was allowing Drupattie's upbringing to take the wrong path, Balgobin left the shop, picking up his old *Raleigh* bicycle, his metal milk cans clattering on the handlebars as he pedaled furiously up Lamaha Street.

Drupattie and I marveled at the wondrous pubescent changes that our bodies were undergoing, the painful lumps that appeared like soft genip seeds under the areolae of our breasts, the slow but sure lengthening of our bodies and faces into those of women. We went into Booker's and bought brassieres somewhat larger than our actual sizes, in happy anticipation of the time when we would finally fill out enough to fit them. Sometimes at night in the dressing case mirror, after my mother and Bernard were asleep, I would look at the slowly rising curve of my hips, rounding thighs and budding breasts and feel the pure quiet joy of burgeoning womanhood.

The last time that 'Gatha had fitted me for a dress, she said to my mother, "Dis gyurl fillin' out yuh know. She gun be a young lady soon." My first menstrual period came in the first year after I had entered high school. My mother had told me the facts of life in graphic detail about a year before this, then gravely talked to me about all the potential dangers for a young girl involved in pre-marital sex. For my part, having been weaned on the experiences of the female protagonists of *True Romance* magazine stories, I felt already well educated in this regard. It did not cross my mind then that my own mother, speaking as she was from personal experience, was as potent an admonitor as any of the heroines of these stories.

"If yuh leh dese boys get close to you, an' yuh get pregnant, *yuh cork duck!*" she said vehemently. "You are a young lady now, an' I expec' you to conduc' yuhself as such. Yuh fadduh in de interior, an' I inten' to keep you in de straight an' narrow. Remember yuh education. Yuh see wha' happen to Shirley? How she always *boxin' from pillar to pos'* an' runnin' rung like a chicken widdout a head? Dat is what does happen to young gyurls who don' keep deh self to deh self. Yuh see how dat good-fuh-nutting Eustace want to marry she an' mek she decent an' she *mekkin' styles pun 'e?* Well I tell you!"

She ended this last bit with an eloquent "Hmmph!"

I felt silent resentment at what I considered to be this gross over-simplification of Shirley's situation. Shirley's abortion had become common knowledge in Lamaha Street and its environs, thanks to the vitality of the village spit press. Some anxious mothers of young girls now used her trouble as an instructive example for their daughters of the possible pitfalls awaiting errant female conduct.

"But Mama," I said. "You see how Eustace treat 'Gatha. Why should Shirley even want to marry him?"

Since I had entered high school and started to grow up, I was becoming more argumentative with my mother.

"Wid de way she does kerry on, Shirley lucky she get even a man like Eustace to *voomps pun she.* She *t'ief* de man from 'Gatha who is a good woman dat was perfec'ly willin' to settle dung wid 'e, an' now she Shirley mekkin styles fuh marry 'e. De two uh dem deserve one anodda," she sniffed, shrugging her shoulders and settling herself more comfortably in the rocking chair into which she usually sank after work.

"But Mama, Shirley didn't *take* Eustace from 'Gatha. Don't you think dat Eustace had some choice in dis?"

With a final "Hmmph!" my mother seemed to indicate that the subject of Shirley and her matrimonial inclinations, or the lack thereof, was closed.

In earlier years on Easter weekend, Bernard and I would go to the seawall to fly our kites which my father had made for us using kite paper, sticks of wood and, to paste the whole thing together, the gum from the sticky *clammacherry* that grew near our home. The seawall location afforded us the full benefit of the north-east trade winds, and as the kites were borne aloft in the breeze over the other young kite-flyers in the crowded seawall area, we would listen for the 'singing' sounds that they made. On Easter Sunday and Monday, the air above the seawall would be abuzz with the sound of kites. Then, as he rarely did, my father would lower his reserve and become a boy again, intent on getting the kites airborne, running between Bernard and me as we manipulated the twine that held them in the air, shouting instructions to each of us, and delightedly taking his turn at flying our kites. My mother, if she could manage a day off from work, would take a picnic basket, and we would all enjoy the time we spent there.

As I grew older, however, I lost interest in kite-flying, and the seawall became the location of other interests. Sunday afternoon excursions there were becoming a habit for some of us girls from my high school, a courting ritual that we thoroughly enjoyed. In groups, we would ride our bicycles along Seawall Road and meet at a certain point near what was called "The Round House," an old colonial kind of look-out point with a view across the Atlantic Ocean. We would dismount, sit on the wall enjoying the north-east breeze that came in from across the ocean and listen to the sounds of local and American popular music that emanated from a juke box in a little shop across the way. Sometimes, too, the British Guiana Police Band would set up its instruments on the bandstand near The Round House and play classical music until it grew dark. Eventually, boys from the various city high schools would also make their way to the seawall and join us. As the sun set over the Atlantic, the boys would eventually pair off with the girls sitting along the seawall. To this day, whenever I hear the roar of the ocean thousands of miles and many, many years away from the pure, simple joy of those Sunday afternoons, I feel a sense of loss.

Steven Osbourne and his friend, Michael Dover, were growing into tall, good-looking young men. It was clear to me that Michael was interested in me, judging from the way his eyes seemed to light up when he saw me as he and his friends came riding along Seawall Road with an affected casualness, their eyes moving down the line of girls sitting on the seawall. In conversations with the group, I was the one at whom he looked, the one to whom most of his remarks seemed to be directed. Steven Osbourne always had a toothpick drooping out of one side of his mouth to give himself an appearance of toughness as he and Michael rode along. Steven was attracted to Drupattie, and even though his friends teased him about liking a *coolie t'ing*, his interest in Drupattie persisted in the face of such racial epithets. He and Drupattie would cuddle on the seawall whispering to each other, and he would ignore his friends' laughing remarks of "Eh! Eh! Wha' happen Steven, man? Like yuh got typee man. Breeze kyan pass between you an' de gyurl."

At seventeen, Michael had the lankiness of youth that

promised to fill out in later manhood. There was a liquid depth to his brown eyes that reminded me of the water in Madewini Creek where we all went swimming during the August holidays. The soothing, mellow tone of his voice evoked my father's when he used to sit with my mother at night on our house's little platform. I would feel a curious quivering within me when I saw Michael, tall and dark brown like *Nugget* shoe polish, and I knew that in some strange way these feelings were associated with the physical changes going on within me. When, from the bar across the way, we heard the Drifters' "Under the Boardwalk," his eyes and mine would meet across the teenage chatter flitting back and forth in the group, and we would know that the song's sentiments were meant for us. His father was a senior Civil Servant; his mother was a housewife, and Michael was one of three children. He had secured a Government County Scholarship in the same year as Steven, and he was still very unsure about what he wanted to do with his life later on.

"I know everyone talks about going away to study some day. It's all Steven talks about, but sometimes I feel that he really jus' wants to get away," he told me, looking out across the Atlantic that roared dully in the distance. "I want to work for a while after I leave school, but my father t'inks it would be a waste of my potential and lack of ambition if I don't go abroad to study. It just seems that too many of those who leave doan come back. I love this place too much never to look back."

"I love it too Michael, but you doan wonder, though, about what lies across that ocean?" I asked him, feeling the cool Atlantic breeze unsettling my pressed curls. "I feel sometimes like I kyan res' till I go and find out. I feel jus' like I'm in a lil house dat kyan hol' me anymore, like I'm in a hula hoop dat's gettin' tighter an' tighter."

The passion in my voice and the north-east breeze had

carried my words down to Belinda Harrison who sat with a group of girls nearby.

"And what makes you t'ink the circle isn't gettin' tighter for Black people across dat ocean, gyurl," Belinda Harrison called out dryly. I did not realize that she had heard me. "If you t'ink Steven got problems seein' an East Indian gyurl here, he should try datin' a white gyurl in the American South."

Michael nibbled my ear and, pulling me closer to him, he murmured jokingly, "Dat gyurl needs a boyfriend. The only t'ing she t'inks about is history and politics. Anyway, if there is anyone who will hold you tighter and tighter, it will be me."

Michael and I had shared our first kiss in that Demerara sunset on the seawall soon after my fifteenth birthday, and later, when we rode our bicycles home, he held my hand all the way, being careful to leave me at the corner of Lamaha and David Streets, a few doors from my home. Along the way, we passed Miss Ida on her way to church, but I was sure she had not seen us. I knew that by nightfall, my mother would be in the rocking chair near the window, crocheting and occasionally looking out for me. I was also certain that she would have been most disapproving of any romantic dalliance that Michael and I engaged in on or off the seawall. Drupattie had ridden home alone behind us because she was afraid to be seen in the village with Steven and was also apprehensive of her family's reaction if they discovered that she had been with a young Black man. I was breathless with pleasure as I ran up the front steps, but as soon as my mother saw me, some primeval maternal instinct in her must have been awakened.

"Miss Lady, you see dis gyallivantin' on de the seawall on a Sunday afternoon?" she asked, looking up at me from the doily she had been crocheting, and then resting it on her lap. "It got to cut dung. Yuh school work come firs'.

De seawall in de night is no place for a decent young gyurl."

Whenever she prefixed her remarks to me with the ominous "Miss Lady," I could be pretty sure that she meant what she said. Even though her announcement startled me, I braced myself for the possibility of an unpleasant future encounter with her on this matter, since I had no intention of reducing my Sunday afternoon seawall activity for such a petty consideration as "female decency." In any event, Michael and I had agreed that we would not let our feelings get the better of us since I, at least, had future plans.

CHAPTER 13

My father was born in a village on the Essequibo River coast in 1919 and came to Georgetown while still a child. His mother was the child of a Black village woman and an immigrant Portuguese shopkeeper who, along with his wife and family, had arrived in the colony from Madeira just before the turn of the century. Grammudduh, who had been raised almost solely by her mother, had married a man who left the village about five years after their marriage and disappeared into the interior of the country with the intentions of seeking his fortune as a *pork-knocker* in the gold and diamond fields—never to return. She struggled alone to raise my father and her two other children, working as a laundress in the village, sometimes walking miles to pick up and deliver clothes to colonial government employees stationed there, or to some villagers like her Madeiran father who could afford to pay to have their clothes laundered.

My father said that he did not remember a time when, as a boy, he did not still feel hungry after eating meals which were always spare and few during his childhood. He told Bernard and me that on Saturdays and during the week after school, he was required to help with the collection and delivery of clothes, walking miles in the heat to his maternal grandfather's house in the village, where often, having entered by the back door, he would stand hungry in the kitchen waiting to be paid for freshly laundered clothes, or to pick up a large basket of dirty laundry. From the dining room of the well-furnished house, the smell of garlic pork, freshly-baked bread and the clink of fine cutlery would mercilessly taunt his appetite; the sounds of conversation in Portuguese would nibble at the edges of his hunger, and he would literally begin to shake.

Sometime near my father's twelfth year, Gramudduh's colonial employer told her that there was an existing vacancy for a laundress at the Catholic hospital then called Colona House in Kingston, a suburb of Georgetown. This administrator was being transferred back to the city, and he hinted that, in exchange for his putting in a good word for her with the Colona House authorities, he would retain her services in his own household when he was back in Georgetown. The work at Colona House was better paying and more secure than the freelance laundressing that she had engaged in on the Essequibo coast during those hard, indifferent years of the early thirties, so early one morning, she took her three children and her few belongings and boarded the bus for the village of Adventure on the Essequibo coast. From there, they got on the ferry boat, the *Lukanani,* heading for the upriver village of Parika, where they took the West Coast railway to Vreed-en-Hoop near the mouth of the Demerara River. By the time that they had crossed the Demerara for Georgetown on the ferry boat called the *Queriman,* it was nearly sunset in the city.

With the help of relatives who had earlier come to the city from Essequibo, my grandmother had pre-arranged to rent two small rooms in one of two range-type dwellings in Robb Street in a part of Georgetown called Lacytown. She and her three children then occupied one half of the structure, while a Portuguese watch-repairer and his family lived in the other. My earliest memories of the *yard* were of periods I spent with my grandmother when I was about three or four years old. The tenants of her building and others in the yard all shared a common outdoor standpipe where all the children bathed and tenants drew water for household activities. For the adults, there was also an enclosed outdoor bathroom made of zinc sheets. In the mornings, the women and girls from the various tenement rooms could be seen making their way to the outdoor latrine to empty their chamber pots and calling to each other.

"Eh, eh, Miss Mildred, how yuh do nuh, gyurl?"

"I here, Miss Bea, t'anks to de will uh de good Lord."

"May-May! May-May! Wake up yuh lazy behine an' bring dung de posy. What yuh waitin' for to empty it? Inspiration?"

(This from Miss Bea to her goddaughter, May-May, who was still sleeping). After they had emptied their chamber pots, the women would gather around the standpipe to wash them and to conduct a daily conference, discussing the possibility of May-May's being pregnant since recently she seemed to be putting on weight and was so tired and sleepy. They would also talk about their plans for the day, what they would buy in the nearby Bourda market, what they would cook for the midday breakfast, and later if there was enough for *bambye*, they would exchange parts of their breakfasts with each other.

The yard was a noisy, active place. The air was intermittently filled with raucous laughter; the playful screams of ragged children whose behavior was the collective responsibility of all the adults in the yard; the occasional curses of a wife whose husband had just returned from a rum shop in Lombard Street; the recorded sounds of the Guianese, Bill Rogers, belting out "Daddy Gone to Cove an' John;" or the Trinidadian calypsonians, Lion, singing "All Day All Night Miss Mary Ann" or Invader, wailing "Rum and Coca-Cola."

Grammudduh rarely experienced the rich life of the yard, being gone from early morning until very late at night working at Colona House and the home of the colonial administrator. Therefore, in her absence, my father, from the age of twelve, had to undertake the care of the two younger children, combing and plaiting my aunt's hair, preparing a meal for them before they all left for school in the morning, and sometimes washing their clothes. Occasionally, my grandmother would bring clothes home to be ironed, and my father and aunt would help her. My aunt who was then eight, would stand on a box at the ironing board, plucking the hot flat irons from the coal pot fire, and stabbing away at the garments late into the night.

At sixteen, my father wanted to leave school to work to help my grandmother, but she insisted that he remain and take the Junior Cambridge exam. He was an insatiable, reclusive reader, and the nuns at his school had told my grandmother that it would be a pity if he did not take the exam which they felt that he had a good chance of passing. Besides, his successful completion of the exam would enable him to get a better paying job than other young men his age. He was very near-sighted, and my grandmother could not afford to buy him glasses, but she had not taken into account the good will and generosity of the yard's occupants. They revered education, and my father was the first among them to take the Junior Cambridge exam. After a standpipe conference, the women took up a collection for his glasses, and his headmaster made up the difference. By July 1939, a few days after my father had taken the exam, my grandmother, underfed and overworked, collapsed of physical exhaustion at Colona House where a doctor there advised her to go home and get some rest, a luxury that she could ill afford because of the scarcity of social assistance for the poor.

I last saw my grandmother when I stopped at her cottage on my way to the airport to fly to the United States where I would enter university. By then she was nearly seventy, stooped after years of bending over a tub, her arthritic hands gnarled, her fingernails broken and blackened by years of prolonged contact with soapy water and scrubbing boards. The olive skin of her face was wizened and wrinkled, and her hair hung in two long, straight, grey plaits down her back. She reached down inside the front of her blouse and withdrew a knotted handkerchief containing a pair of bangles made of solid British Guiana gold. She had been saving for them through the years. When she handed them to me, tears welled in my eyes, for I realized that I would probably never see her alive again, since the uterine cancer with which she had just been diagnosed would probably soon complete the physical destruction begun by poverty.

"Tek dem," she said, as I pushed them back into her hands.

"But Gram," I said. "Dese will do you more good dan me. Keep dem, man."

My voice sounded tight and choked. Her mouth was set in a grim, determined line.

"When yuh go over dat ocean, A want yuh to have somet'ing to remember me wid. Afta rall, you are de firs' born of my firs' born, gyurl. You are a woman now, an' yuh mus' kerry somet'ing of me wid you, somet'ing to keep yuh strong as a woman when you look at it, to let you remember de women yuh come dung from."

Her brown, gnarled hand, closed tightly and firmly over my hand that held the bangles.

I look now at my own soft, delicate hands, just beginning to show the first signs of aging. On my left wrist are the same bangles that I rarely remove; only the middle finger of my right hand is calloused by years of having earned my living by the pen. I am again filled with the emotions of that last meeting over thirty years ago. Grammudduh died two years later, her fingers plucking the sheets of a bed in the Seaman's ward at the Georgetown Hospital. To this day, I can never look at the hands of old, poor, Black women without remembering those of my mother and grandmothers and thinking of the strong threads their fingers often weave into the fabric of Black lives.

Soon after my grandmother had come home sick, my father passed his Junior Cambridge Exam. In 1939, the day before war was declared thousands of miles across the ocean, he applied to the Georgetown Hospital to be trained as a male nurse. He and my mother met at the hospital while waiting, as probationary nurses, to be innoculated against typhoid, another one of the silent, unseen killers of our people.

My mother had grown up in a little village on the West Coast of Berbice. Many of its Black residents were descended from former slaves who had worked on the sugar plantations. My mother was born in late 1919 to a Black laundress who worked on the nearby sugar estate. (Many Black women during this period worked at laundressing, a domestic skill in great demand by white estate overseers and others in the colonial administration). My mother's father was a young Black schoolteacher who taught in the city and periodically visited his parents at West Coast Berbice. When my maternal grandmother realized that she could not work as a laundress and take care of her newborn daughter, she sent the infant to her "in-law's" parents in a nearby village.

My mother told me that her childhood years on the West Coast Berbice were, in many respects, the happiest in her life. There were fruit trees in abundance, carefree playtime, particularly during the August holidays, streams to fish in, and village socials to attend. Her paternal grandparents, who worked as fruit and vegetable farmers, were loving but never overindulgent .

During the August holidays, my mother would go to visit her own mother who, starved for this only child conceived in her later years, would indulge her endlessly. My grandmother shared a cottage with two other women, and when work was scarce on the estate during the economically depressed years of the late twenties and early thirties, the three women formed a kind of informal cooperative unit and shared what work they found. While one woman washed the laundry, another would blue and starch and another would iron. They would then divide equally the little money they managed to make. Sometimes, as they worked, they would sing Anglican hymns to lift each other's spirit. Each could tell the other's mood that day from the hymn that was raised. For example, when Miss Hilda raised "Fight the Good Fight with All Thy Might," the others knew that she was battling depression over absence of the sweet-tongued man who had left her the year before, vanishing into the Rupununi savannahs to work on the cattle trails with a promise to return for her in a month.

My maternal grandmother's cottage was always a hot steamy place filled with the smell of soap and flat irons just removed from the coal pot fire. Often, the women roasted peeled yams or ripe plantains in the coal fire where they also rested the flat irons. They would pluck the hot, delicious food from the glowing ashes with quick, jerking fingers and feed them to my mother, sharing the mothering that momentarily softened the rough edges of their drudgery. At fourteen, my mother was sent to Georgetown to continue her secondary education and to live with her father and stepmother, with both of whom she was largely unfamiliar.

CHAPTER 14

When I was eight years old, Bernard and I were standing with my mother at a bus stop on Regent Street after a matinee at the Metropole cinema where she had taken us. It was about seven-thirty in the evening, and the city seemed to pause and hold its breath, as it often appeared just after sunset when the Demerara shadows were softly descending and deepening.

My mother said to us in a quiet, rather strange voice, "Dat is yuh gran'fadduh's house across de street, yuh know."

I was immediately curious because he had always seemed a shadowy figure, someone whom my mother almost never mentioned, and when she did, only briefly and evasively so. Bernard and I did not know him, but we knew that he and my mother had not spoken to each other in many years.

"Well, let's go over an' talk to him den, Mama," I said, tugging at her hand, and hoping that I would once and for all get to the bottom of the mystery surrounding this man whom I had never seen, not even by way of a photograph. She resisted, telling me that we would miss the Kitty-Regent bus which was already late in coming. Before she could say anything more, I broke from her hand, darted across the street, and found myself knocking on the door of a well kept house. A tall, largish, greying, balding Black man opened the door. His glasses were pulled down his nose a little, the thumb of one hand was hooked into one of his suspenders. He rocked back on his heels, looked down at me over the top of his glasses and said, "Yeh-eh-ess?" He drew out the word, raising his voice at the end. I saw my mother's mouth and chin in his face, her large pensive eyes in his.

I told him my name, adding, "I'm Selina gyurl."

For a moment, he seemed not to understand what I had said, and then he pushed his glasses up on his nose, and looked down at me closely. In my youthful perception of time, it appeared that at least a minute went by as he stared at me blankly, saying nothing.

Just when I was beginning to think that I might as well turn around and go back across the street to face my mother's wrath, he said, his voice trembling slightly, "Where's yuh mudduh?"

"She across de street," I said, turning to point her out. He raised his eyes to look out at her, and then he said, "Come in."

Slowly, mechanically, he took my small outstretched hand and repeated, "Eh! Eh! Suh you are Selina chile." Then he began to chuckle ruefully, rubbing his chin. "Eh! Eh! Well A tell you! Selina chile."

"Well, A have to go," I said after a pause, edging towards the door. "My mudduh is across de street, an' she waitin' on me." I sensed that the only reason why the Selina in question had not come after me was that her anger at my action might have been overruled by her unwillingness to meet her father again. I could feel her eyes fastened on me from the shadows across the street.

"Wait!" he cried, reaching into his pocket. "Take dese two shillin's fuh you an' yuh brudduh. Wait! A will take yuh back."

He took my hand, and we started across the street. Just as we got to the other side, the yellow Kitty-Regent bus, delinquent in its arrival only when it was most needed, pulled up at the bus stop. My grandfather started to say something to my mother.

Indecisively, she seemed to pause briefly, turning slightly to him. But Leon, the bus driver, impatient for the end of his shift, cried out to her, "Hustle up, Nursie! Hustle up! A got lodge meetin' tonight!" In my mind, I damned the unwitting Leon and the belching Kitty-Regent because I thought their arrival would destroy the resolution of conflict my child's heart sensed my mother needed. To me, the activities of Leon's Masonic brothers were of little urgency compared with the possibilities of this moment that was soon lost, swiftly wafted away into the bus' sickening, black, gasolene fumes. My mother grabbed my hand, and she, Bernard and I were barely on the bus before Leon had abruptly slammed shut the door to good intentions.

As we took our seats, my mother looked down at me, livid, and said under her breath, "You *loose* my han' an' tear across de street like dat again, an' A will cut yuh tail good!"

Then changing her tone, she said softly and sadly, her voice catching a little as she stared out into the descending dark, "Some t'ings yuh would'n understan' now. Doan *ever* try to force God han'."

With an energetic movement of his left arm and shoulder, Leon manoeuvered the gear lever into first, and the bus pulled off down Regent Street with a shrill, mournful, almost human wail. Through the back window, I watched my grandfather's figure recede into the soft falling shadows from whence I had briefly plucked him. It would be many years before we would see him again.

With great reluctance, I approach recounting the circumstances that led to my mother's estrangement from her father. One reason is that it has caused her, and consequently me, deep pain. I was constantly conflicted by the fact that, even though my mother's sternness during my childhood and adolescence often resulted in my removing myself from her emotionally, I remained fiercely protective of her in the face of anyone who would harm her. It is only in the course of writing this narrative that I have become comfortable enough to describe in detail the events that led to their estrangement, and even so, I want to be able to do that with some sensitivity for my mother's pain.

During the thirties in British Guiana, very few young Black working women like my mother lived on their own. In the first place, housing was in short supply; few young Black Guianese working people could afford to live independently on the regular wages paid for skilled and unskilled labor: While some young women depended on husbands or child-fathers for support, the majority lived with relatives or hoped that young men with gold rings of "honorable intentions" would come by to rescue them from the "hideous" prospect of endless "spinsterhood." The result was that many young women remained under parental control well into their twenties, often moving directly from their fathers' houses to those of their husbands if an opportunity for marriage presented itself.

When my mother began work as a nurse at the Georgetown Public Hospital in the late thirties, she was put on the regular schedule of six days a week from six in the morning to six at night, for monthly wages of twelve dollars, most of which she had to turn over to her father for "household and other expenses." I sometimes feel that, initially, she reluctantly chose the profession more from expediency than from a deep conviction that nursing was what she really wanted to do. After all, at that time, nursing, teaching or, with greater limitations, the Civil Service, were the main socially acceptable professions in which a young Black woman might engage. My grandfather was anxious that of these three professions, she choose one so that she could be a wage-earning contributor to the household. Even though her passing the nursing entrance examination was a source of pride to them both, it seems to me that she had little choice in the matter of employment.

Soon after the war started, some food items like flour and cooking oil were no longer being imported into the colony. Bicycles, a vital source of independent personal transportation for the colonial working class, were rendered useless by the shortage of rubber used to make tires and inner tubes.

Resourceful citizens substituted rope for tires. Moreover, bicycles were no longer imported because overseas manufacturers devoted their efforts to the production of munitions and other war materiel. Consequently, many workers who could not afford the existing limited public transportation (gasolene was scarce), walked long distances to do demanding six-day twelve-hour labor. In the absence of the modern convenience of elevators in the few three-storied buildings like the Public Hospital, strict British nursing supervisors frequently called on young probationary nurses to "go and bring." Indeed, much of the drudgery fell heavily upon the probationers: lifting and washing patients who could not help themselves; wrapping bodies of dead patients; carrying heavy containers up and down stairs. In addition, in conditions where adequate diet was often impossible for many working people, my mother struggled, along with other young workers in similar circumstances, to adjust to the long demanding hours. She once told me that after her first twelve-hour day, she staggered home from work, dizzy from fatigue and the tropical heat, only to face several household chores that her father and stepmother demanded of her... and always there was the hunger, the gnawing feeling after each spare meal that she wanted more to eat—just a little more that was never there.

The first night of her return home from work, she shivered with fear in the stifling heat as the awful reality of her situation dawned on her. Neither love nor compassion ruled in her father's house, and at work, the noose of unrelenting drudgery and meager wages grew tighter. Employment and life alternatives in the colony were as scarce as bicycle parts. She could not return to her mother in the country: There was no work there, and increasingly young people from the rural areas were coming to the city to try to improve their job prospects. The next day, sore, she dragged herself out of bed and walked back to the hospital again for another day of work.

In recounting her story, my mother would pause and sigh; then she would tilt her head to one side, raise her eyebrows and, shaking her head slowly, would say, "But yuh know? *Yoot'*. Yoot' is a great t'ing if yuh t'ink about it. When yuh body young, it kyan tek a *lotta* strain."

At her father's insistence, my mother went to Adams' for photographs of herself in her nurse's uniform. They were meant to commemorate a milestone of achievement in her life—her first job. My grandfather required that she turn all the photographs over to him, even though she had paid for them from her own earnings. However, before taking the four photographs home and handing them over to my grandfather, she had playfully and flirtatiously shown them to my father who teasingly said, "Well, yuh know, *I* have to get one uh dese!" My mother, thinking nothing of letting him have one, returned home where my grandfather demanded an explanation of why she had only three. When she told him that she had given one to my father, my grandfather flew into a rage and began to beat her first with his fists, then with a stick, calling her vile names and saying that she must get the missing photograph back the next day.

One of his many beatings.

Early the next morning, the side of her face distended and swollen, and her arms splotched with dark purple marks, she rose, packed what she could into a small bag, and tiptoed from the house on Regent Street where he and her stepmother lived.

She really had nowhere to go, so she simply started walking up Regent Street away from the house. Then, a woman did not report such occurrences to the police since it was "naturally" assumed that if as a young woman, you lived in your father's house, he had control over your person. And who were the police themselves but fathers, many of whom shared the same thinking and some of whom did the same things? To some extent, even the colonial authorities themselves shared the culture's patriarchal views. My mother later told me that when she reported the incident to some relatives, they concluded that if her father had beaten her, then he must have had some good reason.

In the period during which she had worked as a nurse, she had absorbed enough of "Anatomy and Physiology" to realize that he had damaged her face. When she tried to move her lower jaw, the pain was intense, and she could not hear out of one ear. She felt as though she were submerged in a water tank. She said that in spite of all this, her overriding fear had been the nursing supervisor's reaction if she reported sick. She could not afford to lose a day's pay now when she would have to pay for a room to rent. Oh God, how would she manage alone? Where would she stay? Everyone knew what people thought of young girls who lived *batchie*. Of one thing she was sure—regardless of how hard it would be to live on her own, she would never, never return to her father's house, nor would she ever again speak to him.

She turned her steps in the direction of the hospital. She would have to report, not for work, but for treatment. Miss Grayson, the stern English supervisor, initially furious that my mother had shown up for work out of uniform, took one close look at her face and exclaimed in a kindly wide-eyed manner (that she had hitherto been careful to conceal from all probationers): "Oh my goodness, dearie! And what in the world happened to you?" Since it was difficult for my mother to talk, the details remained secure from Miss Grayson. (My mother has always insisted that you should "never let white people know yuh business").

She had to be admitted to the hospital, and as her broken jaw mended, she enjoyed all the attention that my father showered on her when he could escape from his own duties as a probationer at the hospital. However, my mother's spirit never recovered completely. Sometimes her eyes would get that soft, sad, distant look seen in the photograph that she and my father took shortly before I was born—the look I saw in them when as children, Bernard and I waited with her at the Regent Street bus stop opposite my grandfather's house and she pensively said to us, "Dat is yuh gran'fadduh's house across de street, yuh know."

After her discharge, she was temporarily able to get a room in the city, and later when her mother came bearing a very small pension from the sugar estate, they rented a tiny one-bedroom cottage on Duncan Street in the village of Campbellville just outside the city.

Then, my father could court her away from my grandfather's oppressive shadow, and in the precious little spare time that they had, they huddled and cuddled in the dark *house* section of the "Metro" or "London" city cinemas, where my mother wept along with Louise Beavers and Claudette Colbert in *Imitation of Life*; where they saw Vivien Leigh and Robert Taylor in *Waterloo Bridge* and Helen Hayes and Clark Gable in *White Sister*.

By 1944, as the war wore on, the British army needed men from the Caribbean. All over the region, young work-

111

ing men like my father saw an opportunity to earn added income and the chance to be part of a military that was a major feature of their male identities and which they had only been able to experience vicariously in war movies they had seen. When his mother's health failed, my father became the family's only breadwinner: His younger brother and sister were still at school. He also decided that some day he would marry my mother, so there was an additional motivation for him to join the army. Some time in 1944, my mother and his family saw him off from a dock in Georgetown. He sailed first to Trinidad and from there on to Barbados, where he became a member of His Majesty's Royal Army Medical Corps. Occasionally, he would return to Georgetown briefly on short leaves.

In September 1945, my mother was on a ferry crossing the Demerara River from Georgetown to the Best Hospital, the colony's tuberculosis sanatorium, where she had been transferred to work. She was leaning on the railings, enjoying the sunrise over the city fast receding in the steamer's wake, and watching the early morning sun glistening, crystalline on the cool Demerara mist. Suddenly she realized that, for the first time in all the occasions when she had crossed the heaving Demerara, she was feeling seasick. Her mouth began to fill with saliva, and before she could control herself, she threw up all over her uniform and the deck.

My father would soon be demobilized, and she had no doubt that he would marry her, but she also knew that it would be financially difficult for them. The colonial authorities required the discharge of all female government employees who became pregnant or who got married. Interestingly, they attached no such stipulations to the conditions of service for fathers- or husbands-to-be.

For various reasons, from the time she first realized she was pregnant until the early months of 1946, my mother kept her pregnancy a secret from all except my grandmothers and my father. She needed to keep her job for as long as possible in order to help my father save for the birth. She also imagined that her pregnancy would provide interesting copy for the spit presses of relatives and others who strongly felt that she should not have left her father's control.

Also, at that time, such stigma was attached to unmarried pregnancy among young women like nurses and teachers in colonial government employ that, in isolated cases, as soon as their condition became visible, some of these young women would take "sick leave" and vanish into the country to live with relatives or family friends. After giving birth, they would leave their babies behind to be reared by trusted others, babies who grew up being encouraged to think of their natural mothers as "sisters," "aunts" or "godmothers." In this way, these young women kept their secrets—and their employment, periodically remitting funds for their children's support. Some independent minded women, rather than risk job loss because of marriage, maintained long term unmarried relationships with men, associations which were conducted through clandestine, sexually intimate meetings in order to preserve the appearance of respectability.

From his salary, my father sent my mother what money he could while supporting his mother and siblings. Meanwhile my grandmothers got together in the cottage and sewed and knitted little soft baby things, talked *ole time story*, and prepared all sorts of milk concoctions like *coague* and *rice pap* to tempt my mother's dwindling appetite while she worked the gruelling hospital schedule, hiding her morning sickness and afternoon drowsiness from the eagle-eyed nursing supervisors.

By May 1946, my father had come home. My mother was thin and exhausted from too little appetite, too much lifting, too much stair-climbing and too much anxiety. My father said that when he saw her waiting for his ship to dock at Booker's wharf on that early May morning in 1946, he started to cry. He barely recognized her. Soon after his arrival, they took the photograph that I earlier described and were married that month.

I was just a few months old when my father was demobilized and finally returned home to civilian life. He and my mother first set up house in the little cottage on Duncan Street. He had left the army with the hope that he would be able to start marriage with the military back-pay that he was due, but getting it from the colonial authorities, as I have related, took his strenuous efforts.

My mother's face is now weathered and lined with the creases of advancing age. Her white hair has grown thinner with every passing year; her shoulders are bowed by arthritis and the weight of the years—fifty of which went into nursing. In the now faded, black and white photograph taken at Adams' in September 1939, the photograph that she had given to my father, I search for her essence in the twenty-year old nurse-girl-woman. Here she stands in sensible black English Oxford nursing shoes, thick beige-colored stockings, long-sleeved pinstripe uniform with close studded white collar, and white nurse's cap, in front of Adam's elaborately painted backdrop of a curved staircase. Her sad, soft eyes and slightly lowered chin belie the steely courage that has always sustained her in the face of life's challenges. Looking at the photograph, I feel the need to protect, comfort and draw her to me, sensing that even before I had been physically conceived, my own spirit had already been joined with her bruised soul.

CHAPTER 15

"'Mama look a boo-boo!' dey shout.
Dey muddah tell dem, 'Shut up yuh mout'!
Dat is yuh daddy.' 'Oh no!
My daddy kyan be ugly so.'"

On radios all along Lamaha Street, the voice of the calypsonian, Lord Melody, could be heard on a Saturday morning radio program belting out the lyrics to his popular hit. The rainy season was slowly coming to a close, and the sun struggled futilely to get through, burning away the smell of rain-soaked earth that had hung over Kitty for many days. Yards had been flooded, and even the village madwoman, Banga Mary, who talked to herself incessantly and made it a habit in good weather to sleep on old sugar bags and assorted rags under the awning of Mr. Jacobs' shop, had disappeared whither no one knew.

Thunder had rumbled intermittently over the village for days, and there was talk of an impending hurricane, as people reminisced expectantly about Hurricane Janet that had earlier devastated neighboring islands in the Caribbean. We had heard Mr. Braithwaite cursing his family for many nights, and in a crescendo of loud, drunken eloquence, he had proclaimed that Gwennie and her mother were "amalgamated whores." My mother suggested to Gwennie that she should stay at our house so that she could get some sleep, but she preferred to remain at their own cottage to try to protect her mother.

At about seven-thirty one morning, the last of his nights

of verbal abuse, Mr. Braithwaite started to throw his wife's and children's belongings out into the muddy yard, demanding that they leave. But they had nowhere to go. Eventually, Mr. Jacobs, hearing the commotion, closed his shop, and meandered through the gathering crowd of onlookers on the street outside the house. He walked into the yard, glancing occasionally up into the cottage to ensure his own safety, and started to help Joe-Joe, Winston and a tearful Gwennie pick up their scattered clothing and other odds and ends. He told the children that he would let them all stay temporarily in the spare room at the back of his shop until Mr. Braithwaite's drunken fit was over.

But there was an air of finality to their departure. In his earlier drunken tirades, Mr. Braithwaite had always been an object of derision on Lamaha Street, but everyone usually assumed that these were passing and that, at the end of each spell, he would return as usual to the dignified, but morose and brief sobriety that he always embraced like a grim unwelcoming mother—periods when no one dared hold him in scorn and everyone called him "Mr. Braithwaite." However, there was a new twist to his behavior: His drunken spells lengthened ominously as his life entered into a viciously tightening circle. As work was denied him because of his chronic alcoholism, that condition worsened accordingly. I trembled at the horror at which he stared, so terrifyingly palpable to him but invisible to all of us, a horror that would cause him to discard, like old *Chronicle* newspapers, the people who were closest to him.

He let Joe-Joe and Winston take Mrs. Braithwaite's sewing machine and chiffonier. The onlookers watched quietly from the street as the boys lifted the scarred, stained chiffonier down the rickety front steps, its cracked glass doors sometimes swinging open like suppliant hands. I helped Gwennie with two bags, one a battered cardboard suitcase that Mr. Braithwaite had used for his trip to

Wembley and another bag which contained some of the chiffonier's tea things that she and I used to play with when we were younger.

Suddenly, we heard a thud at our feet. Mr. Braithwaite had thrown his wedding photograph after them. His wife bent slowly to retrieve it from the mud in its broken, smudged frame, and the picture of the sober, youthful workman and the vibrant, young seamstress stared back at us from the shadows of the past, their eyes full of promise and bright with hope. Mrs. Braithwaite's hands moved gently over his face in the photograph, hands that in good health had sewn for a living all day and well into the night.

I was standing behind Mrs. Braithwaite and did not know that she had been crying until I saw her tear fall, with a soft, barely perceptible sound, upon her husband's face in the photograph. At that moment, I felt a fierce rage at Mr. Braithwaite that threatened to choke my young soul. The brevity of my years then did not permit me to see that human love can be frail and, for all its immense capacity to strengthen and exalt the human spirit, is itself still disturbingly vulnerable to misfortune and caprice.

In his backroom, Mr. Jacobs provided an old bed on which Gwennie and her mother would sleep, while the boys would spend their nights on bedding on the floor, the same kind that Mr. Jacobs had given to Banga Mary to make her nights under the awning more comfortable. A week later, her youth abbreviated at fifteen like a seamstress' mistaken cut of a hem, Gwennie left school and started to work as a maid for a member of a foreign High Commission. She left early in the morning and returned late at night, sweating and exhausted. Sometimes, depending on the needs of her employer, she was gone for days, so that I no longer saw her as much as I used to. One afternoon after school, while I was sipping a milkshake and chatting with some school friends at the soda fountain in Booker's, I saw her, but ignoring the fact that our eyes had met, she turned away and disappeared into the crowd on the pavement outside.

Joe-Joe and Winston "hustled" about the village, sometimes suspected, but never openly accused, of one or other nefarious activity: One day Miss Oz lost a white Rhode Island fowl cock that she had been fattening for Mr. Osbourne's birthday, and it occurred to her that she saw Joe-Joe's figure disappearing in the dawn darkness over the palings of her back fence when she had awakened on hearing her fowls cackling uneasily under her house; Mr. Sampson, the cabinet maker, lost several two-by-fours from his shop one rainy night and, next morning, discovered Winston's sodden cap near the gate of his premises. Sometimes, when we rode past them on our way from school, Joe-Joe and Winston would be sitting on the railings of a *bridge* to some village shop with toothpicks or smoking *Lighthouse* cigarettes dangling from the sides of their mouths. They would call out obscenities to Drupattie and me, slamming Drupattie with the ethnic slur of "coolie water-rice" and indicating what they would like to do to us if they could strip us of our school uniforms and tackle us on the other side of the seawall. We would ignore them, putting our noses in the air, holding on to the crowns of our Panama hats as we pedaled away.

CHAPTER 16

It had been nearly three years since Shirley set up house with Eustace. He pestered her continually to marry him, but she firmly refused. Often, on my way from school, I would stop by their cottage, and she and I would sit on her backsteps eating genips and spitting out the seeds as she set her hair with paper curlers, painted her toenails, shelled shrimp, cleaned fish or did some other chore in preparation for Eustace's dinner. I never told my mother about these after-school detours because I knew that she would not approve. She and other women in the village who knew Shirley thought that her refusal of Eustace's offer, even as she continued to live with him, bordered on a kind of perverse indecency. In the eyes of Shirley's critics, 'Gatha was spared such criticism because she had at least been eager to marry him. Furthermore, in my mother's words, Shirley was "a woman of the world," "sheer trouble,"—in other words, a bad influence on my impressionable pubescence. Of course, it was an open secret that Shirley continued to see Cromwell, and this, a matter that no one dared mention to Eustace, did nothing to improve my mother's impression of Shirley.

"But why you wun marry he?" I would ask Shirley. "It seem to me like he really like you. Afta rall, is over two years, an' it look like 'e treatin' you good."

"*Pickney*," she would say with weary patience, using part of the creole folk saying, *"You a come; you a come.* You marry a man like Eustace, or leh dem feel dat you dyin' to marry dem, an' deh treat you like dog dung under deh shoe after deh put dat ring t'rough yuh nose. You see wha' 'e do wid 'Gatha? Dat en gun happen to me."

"But Shirley," I insisted, forgetting my own earlier conviction that Eustace would make a most unsuitable husband. "You as good as married to him now. What about if you get pregnant?" Of course, prompted by my former extensive *True Confessions* readings, I felt entitled to push for a "happy ending."

Her jaw tightened then, and her eyes and voice took on a strange hardness that seemed to permeate her very core.

"I doan want chirren, an' I doan want husban'," she said with bitter emphatic finality. "A want me fuh me. Woman get chirren an' husban' an' like she lose sheself. She belong to diff'ren' people, an' she have nutting lef fuh sheself. I look about me. I look at 'Gatha how she nearly lose sheself. A look at me own mudduh how she already lose sheself, an' I seh man can keep 'e ring. You see Auntie Edna an' Auntie Ida? Deh poor, but deh hol' on to dehself, gyurl. At firs' ah use to laugh at dem, but ah learn. In dis mudflat, de men doan even own deh-self, an' deh hustlin' to own you de woman. Some uh dem en even got a posy to pee in, but deh hustlin' to lord it over you de woman. Who de hell dead an mek dem king?"

She spat out a genip seed with scornful force. I had no answer for this since, until then, I had never seriously considered matters of adult female experience. Besides, I had never before heard a woman speak so contemptuously about affairs that were generally accepted as being part of a woman's natural existence.

After a brief silence, I said quietly, "What if 'e fine out 'bout Mr. Cromwell?"

It was the first time that I ever revealed to her that I had heard she was still seeing Cromwell. She was silent for a few moments; then she replied just as quietly as I had asked the question, "Den so be it. Jus' like man mus' do wha' 'e mus' do, woman mus' do to."

Something in her voice, the yawning distance in her eyes—as though she had entered some strange foreign country across the ocean where she could not be reached—sent a feverish shiver down my spine.

A northeasterly breeze rattled the leaves of the coconut tree in the backyard, and it too seemed to shiver sympathetically; a large carrion crow circled overhead, and from a neighbor's radio came the mellifluous tones of Nat King Cole singing *"Non Dimenticar."*

One night about a week later, I was in the living room studying for one of Miss Burgess' Latin tests. My mother had started to put out her houseplants to catch any moisture of dew or rain that might accumulate that night. In what was a nightly ritual for as long as I could remember, she lumbered from the living room to the landing and back again, putting out first her 'hassar backs,' then her 'mother-in-law tongues.' She was humming "I Love You for Sentimental Reasons" and putting as much feeling into it as possible, sometimes fussily touching the leaves of the plants as if they were her children.

It was just after nine o'clock, and the male announcer's voice on the radio intoned the death announcements:

"... died at her residence at Hadfield Street,
Werk-en-Rust. She was the beloved mother of Tobias
of the Deeds Registry; sister of Isaac, retired from
the Transport and Harbours Department; grandmother of eight, great-grandmother of five. Funeral
services will be held tomorrow afternoon at four at
St. Philip's Church, and thence to the Le Repentir cemetery for burial. The death is announced of... "

and so on through sometimes as many as ten or more death announcements read against the mournful background of some organ dirge.

Suddenly, the sound of agitated voices and running footfalls on Lamaha Street caught our attention. From the dimly lit street, we heard fragments of loud, excited comments repeated from one person to the other, each of whom seemed to be running in the same direction up the street. "...Gyurl geh kill up de road... " "Deh call police arready..." "She bring it pun sheself..."

Bernard and I shoved away our books, and my mother quickly dropped the 'maidenhair' fern that she had just been handling gingerly. Some nagging suspicion propelled me out the front door and down the front steps, Bernard following quickly behind. We ignored my mother's cries for us to stay indoors and fled down the street, joining the rushing crowd of villagers.

We came upon the point where they converged, and I squirmed my way through the crowd to the front of the growing circle of people. There, on the street under the dim lamplight lay the slight, still body of a woman, face up, head tilted to one side, arms outstretched as in crucifixion. A long stream of blood snaked like a black *camoudi* from under her. The front of her blouse was soaked with blood, and her skirt was up to mid-thigh exposing her legs, one of which was slightly bent, while the other stretched straight downwards. Blood oozed from gashes on her right arm, the cut flesh looking like raw meat. There was a high-heeled shoe on her left foot, while the other shoe lay discarded nearby. Rufus and the other stray dogs had gathered, yapping and running excitedly around the body, sometimes pausing to lick at the stream of blood as their tails swiped the air like whips.

I broke from the crowd, and edging closer, braving the sickeningly rank smell of blood, I recognized Shirley lying in the dust. I screamed and, nauseated, my mouth filling with saliva, I staggered back right into my mother's arms, feeling my knees beginning to buckle.

As though from a distance I heard the comments of some in the crowd.

"'E finally ketch up wid she," said Miss Priscilla in a loud, emphatic whisper.

She was a large woman also familiarly known as Miss Priss, who sold fish in the market.

"She had it comin' to she," replied another. *"She eye pass de man."*

"Dis is wha' you get when you want to play a street 'oman," Miss Olga sharply whispered to her young niece, Verone, who, at twelve, was particularly well developed physically and had shown a precocious tendency to flirt with young men in the area.

I felt sweat beginning to form like Demerara dew on my forehead. My mother was pulling me away, urging me home, but I wrenched myself away violently in open defiance of her. Surprisingly, she left me alone, relenting quietly, and remained with me on the inner edge of the ring of people around Shirley's inert form.

Later, we learned from Burchell, the postboy, the details of the events that led to the murder. In the course of beating an arrestee in the lock-ups, Eustace was surprised by the miserable devil's taunt that he (Eustace) could not even "control 'e woman," that Shirley had been *"gi'in' 'e blow,* an' meetin' a man at the Arawak Hotel on the East Coast." Eustace received the information without comment or any sign that he was at all affected by the news. He dealt the handcuffed man a parting kick with all the force of his muscular frame, hitched up his black policeman's serge pants, and stomped out of the lock-ups, his heavy boots thumping ominously on the wooden floor. Had he not given Shirley all she wanted, even to the point of denying his own children? Put food in her belly, clothes on her back? I imagine that he stepped out into the Alexander Street sunshine filled with rage at the thought that she had turned to someone else.

He loved her with a feverish, relentless passion that he had never before felt for a woman. There was something about her that, as he had told Burchell, nullified his attraction to other women: the hint of the smell of breast milk in her dusky skin, something indefinable in the corridors of his consciousness that harkened back to an infantile period before his intellect was fully formed, when he had clung to his mother, who died of malaria just before he was two years old. The soft, vulnerable curve of the back of her neck, the tight smoothness of her upper arms, the casual mellowness of her voice—all locked him in a circle of pleasurable, but disturbing emotion. With the other women he had known, his attraction ultimately dried into irritated boredom and free-floating hostility, but Shirley stirred in him a bottomless well of desire from which he drank but was never sated. Yet, even as he loved her, he hated the feeling of helplessness that accompanied the emotion, the feeling that he was becoming as love-besotted as 'Gatha whom he had spurned.

Shirley's refusal to marry him or bear his children stung his pride like a deep, lingering *marabunta* bite, and this rejection became a challenge that he felt forced to overcome either by gifts or by guile. No other woman had ever refused him; even dat 'Gatha who di' like to run 'im up an' dung court steps would jump to have 'im now if 'e tackle 'er. Walkin' pass 'im in de village wid she nose in de air like somebody dead an' mek she queen!

He remained plagued by his suspicions, saying nothing to Shirley, quietly biding his time. A knot of resentment must have settled in his stomach as he thought of Cromwell. Cromwell, the smooth, "respectable" Civil Servant, the one with the education and prospects, who did not have to dirty his hands with the criminal poor.

One afternoon, Shirley said that she was going to see

Carmen Jones at the "Globe" cinema, and Eustace offered her a lift on his bicycle. She agreed. He saw her into the building and said that he was going to meet some friends to 'chop some dominoes' in Charlestown. She told him not to pick her up at the end of the show, that she would take the Kitty-Regent home. Two hours later, Eustace was returning from the game and stopped for a *Banks* beer at Mr. Jacobs' shop and to *gyaff* with some village men who usually talked politics there until late into the night. After about an hour, he got on his bicycle and began to pedal home when he saw the blue *Vauxhall* turn into Lamaha Street at the corner up ahead of him.

Something about the car's snaking crawl to a slow stop caught his policeman's attention. Then somewhere in the recesses of his investigator's memory, there stirred the description of the car Mrs. Cromwell drove that Saturday morning over two years before when she had attacked Shirley. He stopped in the darkness, watching the parked vehicle, and then crept quietly up behind it. In the dim light of the corner street lamp, he recognized Shirley and Cromwell.

He waited in the darkness while Shirley got out of the car, bent down to the open window, kissed Cromwell long and lingeringly and called out sweetly and softly to him, "Night night, darlin'." He heard Cromwell's curt baritone reply of "Sleep tight." He was not at all anxious to be spotted letting Shirley off so close to her home. Leaving her standing on Lamaha Street, the car roared away into the night with a seemingly human wail.

Suddenly, with the unintelligible cry of a wounded animal, an enraged Eustace was upon her. He withdrew from inside his shirt the hunting knife that he always carried since he was attacked one night by one of his victims, newly released from the Georgetown Prison on Camp Street. Eustace stabbed her, silently plunging the knife three times into her upraised right forearm. She screamed, "Murder! Murder! Oh God, Eustace! Oh God! Somebody come quick! Oh God!" Her screams were cut short by a last frothy gurgle of blood rushing up to her lips from her lungs, after he had plunged the knife deep into her chest and stomach.

Miss Oz had been settling down for the night when, always alert to sounds in the night, she thought she heard a woman's scream. She looked out her gallery window and saw the two individuals tussling in the light of the street lamp. By the time she reached the street, herself screaming, Shirley had fallen, the last moments of her life ebbing in a snaking stream of blood in the dust. Eustace had vanished in the darkness.

Miss Oz's screams alerted the residents along the street, who now gathered in a wide, agitated, quietly chattering circle around the body. Soon the police van drew up, screeching to a halt nearby, and the crowd made an opening in the circle like a gaping mouth, to receive three local constables and Police Superintendent Nelson Irving. An Englishman and member of the colonial administration, he was starchly dressed in uniform khaki. In his presence, the crowd slowly hushed.

"Does anyone know this gehl?" he asked, his clipped, English tones sounding surreally inconsonant with the setting.

Silence... . Even the local constables who must have known of the relationship between Shirley and Eustace did not reply.

"Does anyone know this gehl?" he repeated, this time slowly and distinctly, as though he thought we could not understand Standard English. Again, silence... . "Does anyone know who did this to her?"

A slightly shrill impatience tinged the tone of his last question. It reminded me somewhat of Mr. Davis' attempts to ferret out the culprit when some yet undiscovered child in the scholarship class had committed a misdeed.

Miss Priss piped up respectfully, "No sir. We doesn't know her, sir. We wasn't dare, sir."

Irving, an alien to people alien to him, people he would never fully understand for all the twenty years he had spent in the colony, went around the crowd repeating his questions, but the villagers had formed a hard ring of defence against his starched khaki authority. Suddenly, Banga Mary, the village madwoman, broke from the crowd and, with fierce rasps, tearfully chased away Rufus and the other dogs. Her toothless jaws made empty, agitated, chewing movements as she tenderly covered Shirley's body with the rags on which she herself slept.

After he had killed Shirley, Eustace made his way to a room that Burchell rented in a house near the East Coast train tracks. Alarmed at Eustace's blood-splattered appearance, Burchell at first thought his friend had been attacked. However, he soon learned the details of the incident from a distraught Eustace, details that Burchell would later share with the police and everyone else he encountered as he made his daily postal rounds.

He said he had urged Eustace to go to the police, to confess everything, to throw himself upon the mercy of the law. Afta rall, Burchell reasoned, it was what dem big time lawyers an' dem call "a crime of passion." De woman di' deserve it. Afta rall, she di' *hornin'* 'e. An' to besize, as 'e was a policeman, dey might not treat 'im in de usual way. Eustace was familiar with the misery of incarceration: He had generated a good deal of it. The thought of spending his life, completely vulnerable, among some of those he routinely and callously abused, filled him with an unfamiliar fear. He was fairly sure that Miss Oz had recognized him, and, even if she hadn't, he would surely be a prime suspect: He had the opportunity (the men at Mr. Jacobs' shop could place him near the scene of the crime close to the time when it had been committed), and he was sure time would reveal he had the motive. Finally, the police themselves would be able to attest to the fact that he had the temperament for the commission of such a crime. The harder Eustace thought about it, the more he was convinced that there was no way out of his situation.

According to Burchell, Eustace felt remorse, not for killing Shirley, but for doing it so impulsively, without considerable premeditation. The next morning, he left Burchell's room, and as the seven-fifteen train came down the tracks from Rosignol, he hurled himself into its path.

CHAPTER 17

About a week after Shirley's death, she was buried in the Le Repentir cemetery. Immediately after the murder, the police had taken temporary possession of the corpse because an autopsy had to be performed to determine the cause of death. When Superintendent Irving told Miss Ada and her sisters of this legal necessity, Miss Ada *steupsed* her teeth and told Irving that he and de law mus' be damn fools if till now dey din know how de gyurl get she dead. "An' to t'ink dat alyou wun even leh she res' in peace even now!" Miss Ada had screamed-sobbed at a red-faced spluttering Irving and the local policemen in the station, who watched in gaping astonishment, having never heard any local person talk to the Superindent in anything but tones of implied genuflection.

The night before the burial, Miss Edna, Miss Ada and Miss Ida held a wake at their cottage. Neighbours came in the late afternoon, bringing food, bottles of mauby, ginger beer and sorrel. Some were sad, others stern in grief and sympathy, but all were hushed. Some of the women helped Miss Ada and Miss Ida lay out and prepare the food, while the men, including Mr. Braithwaite, Burchell, Mr. Osbourne, Balgobin, Ragunandan, Mr. Jacobs and the usual group of hangers-on at his shop, sat around under the cottage, talking quietly and drinking rum and water from little snap glasses that Miss Edna had carefully removed from her "shuvoneer" for the occasion. Bahadur, the market grocer, had sent Bissoon, his young East Indian helper, with a large box of groceries. Bissoon, loathe to return to the monotony of his chores for Bahadur, hung around on the fringes of the group of men under the house, furtively sipping rum from a snap glass that someone had offered him. Miss Ada, usually a physically robust woman, had lost weight; her cotton dress hung loosely around her hips; her breasts sagged; her shoulders were rounded and drooping, her eyes red-rimmed, and her face pinched and tight with grief.

Miss Oz put an arm around her and murmured gently, glancing deferentially at the impassive face of the blue-eyed Jesus on the sitting room wall, "Y'know gyurl, yuh have to put yuh trus' in de Lord. Only he know why dis had to happen. An' Shirley was such a *nice* gyurl to!"

Miss Ada began to sob quietly, her shoulders bowed and shaking.

"Oh yes," Auntie Joycie echoed sweetly and feelingly. She had been among those who had witnessed Mrs. Cromwell's attack on Shirley. "A nice gyurl, a nice, *nice* gyurl."

"Is true! True-true! True-true!" endorsed Miss Mavis, Auntie Joycie's helper in her cake-shop across the street.

"I always does tell me husban' dat dere is a reason why God does leh dese t'ings happen." This from Miss Priss.

"Is true," added Miss Ida, "Is His divine will. Gyurl, His han' in evert'ing. None of us big enough to know what is in His mine. No one know de day or de hour, an' *time longer dan twine!*"

In the sitting room, Miss Edna sucked her teeth, stopping abruptly in her arrangement of the pulourie Drupattie's mother had sent.

"All I got to tell yuh all more-holy-dan-righteous is dat if is de Lord will dat Shirley dead like dis, den I doan want de Lord, an' de Lord not welcome to Shirley. If is his will, den de Lord doan love Ada, an' 'E doan love Ida, an' 'E doan love me, an' 'E surely din love Shirley!" she cried passionately.

The warm, uneasy silence in the room threatened to smother us all. My mother shifted her weight uncomfortably in the Morris chair. The corners of Miss Priss' mouth tightened noticeably and drooped. Auntie Joycie, who was eating a pine tart and was about to take another bite, looked like she was going to choke.

Miss Ida was aghast. Had Edna lost her mind? After the murder, Edna had had the nerve to speak with such disrespect to Superintendent Irving that Ida was sure it was only Irving's sympathy for Ada's grief that prevented him from charging her with disorderly conduct. Now here she was, flyin' in de face uh de Lord 'Eself! When would dis sacrilegious woman stop 'er blasphemy? De Lord was already punishin' dem all fuh Shirley behaviour. Ada cun' see dat? Lord have mercy on de pore fool!

But Miss Edna was encouraged by the attention she had attracted and also emboldened by a stiff shot of rum Mr. Osbourne had urged upon her to lift her spirits. Her voice cut the silence like her sharp black pudding knife.

"Wha' mek alyou t'ink dat anybody out deh hearin' we when we cry 'Lord, Lord?' Look at how we all have fuh struggle fuh mek en's meet! Every day is a battle! Wha'ever Shirley de di' do, she din deserve fuh dead like a stray dog in de street!"

She waved her arms as she spoke, splashing some of the rum on the floor. Silence in the living room. Then from under the house came Mr. Braithwaite's mournful drunken tenor, raised in a slow rendition of the hymn, "What A Friend We have in Jesus." A fly lighted on a crumb on the plastic tablecloth in the living room, alternately eating and rubbing its two front legs together. Then it flew off and settled on Jesus' impassive face, exploring His blond hair, running over His blue eyes, pausing on the nail wounds on His outstretched hands, returning to His face, seeming to demand of Him answers to questions that no one but Miss Edna dared raise.

The funeral took place on the afternoon of the next day, Sunday, at Miss Ida's little ramshackle church, which was packed with friends, relatives, and curious onlookers, many of whom stood outside and whispered. They had read the *Daily Chronicle's* front page account of the murder under the lurid alliterative caption, "Constable Kills Common Law Companion," with its sub-title, "Successful Suicide Bid." The newpaper carried a photograph of Eustace in uniform taken at Adam's Studio the day after he had joined the police force. His officer number, 0666, was faintly visible in the photograph. He held his head high; his eyes stared levelly into the camera. There was an account of his early years, reference to "his now abbreviated promising career" and the important role he had played in the maintenance of law and order before he had "become involved in the tragic situation that finally ended his young life." There was also a blurred photograph of Shirley, "a city waitress of ill repute," wearing an off-the-shoulder dress, a glass in one hand, a cigarette in the other, standing with a group of friends at the Blue Lantern, an establishment to which the *Chronicle* referred as a "shadowy backstreet tavern in Tiger Bay." More space had been devoted to speculation about Shirley's "secret adulterous liaison with an unnamed married Civil Servant" and the "tragically gruesome" nature of Eustace's suicide than to the murder.

In the little church, Shirley lay strangely peaceful and small, dressed in white like a bride. 'Gatha had volunteered to sew the burial dress, and some villagers helped with the funeral expenses incurred at Woo Ming's funeral parlor. The Chinese undertaker's Black assistant was nicknamed "Spongedown" because he was charged with washing the corpses. To replace death's grimace, he had tried to fashion a smile on Shirley's face and had placed her hands together in a posture of prayer.

Spongedown usually slept at night in one of the empty coffins in the funeral parlor. One night, years previously, after having been awakened by thieves who had broken into the backroom where Woo Ming kept his safe, Spongedown suddenly sat up in a coffin in the darkened funeral parlor. The sight of his silhouetted rotund torso coming upright out of the coffin had been enough to scare away the thieves or any others who had similar future plans. Woo Ming, grateful for Spongedown's fearlessly willing presence in the parlor at night, kept the former derelict in his employ for many years thereafter.

Some of Shirley's relatives in the country had been summoned to the funeral by messages relayed over Radio Demerara: "Calling Fitzwilliam Barclay, also known as Uncle Fitzie of Alness Village, Courentyne. Your niece, Shirley, is dead. Come quickly. This message is sent by Edna." Shirley's relatives decided to adhere to African-Guianese tradition and so, from hand to hand, they passed Shirley's infant cousin over the coffin. The frightened screams of the two-year old were joined with the wailing of other relatives and the congregation's mournful drone of "Abide With Me, Fast Falls the Evening Tide."

After having ascertained Shirley's name from Miss Ada just seconds before he assumed the pulpit, the minister, a good-looking young man who had been receiving training in the evangelical ministry, alluded several times in his brief sermon to "our dear departed sister, Shirley." Without explicitly speaking of the circumstances of her death or referring to her specifically, he exhorted the young women present not to fall into the devil's trap of fornication and adultery set at every turn to ensnare and destroy our young lives. He urged us to walk in the straight and narrow path of the virtuous woman whose price is beyond rubies, to give our lives to Jesus and to become His brides.

Amidst the shrieks of the women, Shirley's male relatives, led by Uncle Fitzie, bore the body from the church, their battered leather shoes dragging falteringly through the *Bourn-Vita* colored mud in the yard. The Le Repentir cemetery ground was slushy that day, its stately palms standing like indifferent giant sentinels lining the path to eternity, as the coffin made a splash in the watery grave. I threw onto the coffin a red hibiscus flower that I had picked from my mother's garden. Shirley loved hibiscuses, and she had always liked to arrange them in empty jars in her cottage, but always shortlived, by nightfall, they would close and wilt after their earlier daytime beauty. Later, as most people drifted away to wash the bad luck of *buryin' grung* mud off their shoes, my mother raised the hymn, "We Will Meet at Jesus' Feet," and Miss Ada, Miss Ida and she huddled at the graveside, their voices raised in soprano tremor, their forms silhouetted against the fast growing tropical dusk, as the mud-splattered grave diggers heaved the last remains of rain-soaked earth onto the coffin. Miss Edna, her lips unmoving, stood stonily, slightly apart from the women singing at the graveside.

When we finally left Shirley to her foremothers, it was darkening fast. Still, I could dimly discern the now familiar blue *Vauxhall* edging its way slowly along one of the Le Repentir side roads. My mother and the other women were so engaged in conversation that they did not notice it. The car came to a stop near the deserted, fresh gravesite, and the bent figure of James Cromwell emerged. I paused to watch his bowed, motionless form standing at the graveside, the image slowly being devoured by the darkness. My mother's voice yanked me back from my absorption: "Come along gyurl! You seein' *jumbie* or what?"

For the first time in my life, death had stared back at me out of the face of someone I knew closely. Shirley's murder sprang a leak in my small existence that threatened to throw me off course, to run me aground on the hard rocks of depression. Months after, I would sit in the classroom, gazing distractedly out into Murray Street's dazzling Demerara sunshine. I did not notice the procession of pedestrian, bicycle and car traffic that streamed by on its way to the downtown area of Georgetown, nor did I hear the monotonous choral drone of Latin verbs emanating from the students who sat beside me. Pausing as she intently worked her way through the subjunctive mood, Miss Burgess would sometimes sharply rap me back to attention.

"Young lady," she would begin with faintly disguised sarcasm, drawing herself up to her full height, her shiny, pressed curls glinting a little menacingly. "Do you seriously intend to pass the General Certificate of Education, Ordinary Level?"

Why, oh why couldn't she say "the G.C.E., 'O' Level" like everyone else? Why, when she knew my name, did she always call me "young lady?" How could I tell her about Shirley, bleeding slowly to death under the village street light as the dogs first sniffed then lapped her blood? Where in Miss Burgess' world of conjugations and declensions, of classical foreign education and cocktail parties at the Georgetown Club was there tolerance for the likes of someone like Shirley? She was part of the great Black unwashed, an embarrassment to the colony's "good Black people," who, armed with academic achievement and social standing, tried to rise above colonial contempt and present themselves as fit subjects of the mother country. Shirley who, like a *sakkiwinky* with a broken limb, had tried to soar above the tightening circle, to live her life as she saw fit, giving full vent to her emotions, free of the restraints the pretentious middle class imposed on themselves.

Sometimes, I feigned interest in the subjunctive presented in a Latin account of Caesar's invasion of Britain, an account which Miss Burgess read in fluent conversational Latin as though it were a living language. For weeks afterwards at the end of the school day, I went to Shirley's cottage and sat on the back steps, watching the wind zeg through the branches of the coconut tree in her backyard.

No one came near the closed-up cottage now. A neighbor swore that, as God was her witness, one night she had heard Eustace calling out Shirley's name just as he always did when he approached the gate after work. Another was sure that late one night, she had heard Shirley singing "Que Sera, Sera."

CHAPTER 18

Reflecting on it now, I can only say that Shirley's death at the end of 1961 was a turning point in my sobering journey towards womanhood. Her death and its circumstances, the experiences of Gwennie, her mother, 'Gatha, Balgobin's daughters, Lilowtie and Chandrowtie, Ada, Ida and Edna, and even those of my own mother and grandmothers led me to reflect on my worth and prospects as a "coloured girl in the ring," a woman in our culture. I realized that, as much as our women were nurtured and supported by some of their cultural experiences, they were tyrannized and spiritually devastated by others. Furthermore, whatever the moral judgments that Shirley's style of living elicited, she had paid a terrible and undeserved price. I thought that perhaps the only way to control my destiny, to secure my sense of self as a woman—to *feel* my life—was to escape the ring, to go abroad and seek education beyond the mudflat. However, for all their allurements, the alien shores that attracted me were as daunting as my own culture was unforgiving of its women who dared seek self. Even though I could not adequately articulate it at the time, I was perplexed by how to secure who I was and who I wanted to be as a woman without sacrificing my culture, my motherland.

I felt there was more taking place in me besides the biological transformation associated with puberty. I experienced an awakening in my awareness of the complexities of adult experience that awaited me, an awareness which, coincidentally, was joined with developments occurring in the political arena of British Guianese life.

Looking west from Kitty towards the capital on February 16, 1962, we saw huge columns of black smoke that billowed upward all afternoon and on into sunset, as parts of the capital city burned. Bernard and I urged my mother to let us go down to the city to see the fires, but she adamantly refused: We were not even allowed to leave the yard.

The year before this, the East Indian dentist-politician had won the election he contested against the largely Black-supported Chief. The following three years brought intense political and racial strife to British Guiana. The minority status of African-Guianese left many feeling politically marginalized and dominated by the majority East Indian population. Where formerly many African-Guianese and East Indian Guianese felt united by a common legacy of colonial exploitation and lived together fairly peacefully in the capital city and the villages, increasingly now, even in Kitty, they succumbed to ethnic animosity. Back and forth, both sides hurled ominous racial epithets of "nigger," "kaffir" and "coolie." I shuddered at the prospects for Drupattie and Steven Osbourne's relationship.

Large numbers of African-Guianese rallied around the Chief and sometimes used the broom, his party's symbol, as an offensive weapon during street skirmishes with East Indian opponents in the fiercely contested elections of that blistering August of 1961. Joe-Joe and Winston now rode menacingly about the village on old stolen bicycles, each with a *pointer* broom laid across its handlebars. Both boys sometimes called out threateningly to Balgobin as he returned home after his milk rounds, or to Bissoon as he went about the business of delivering groceries. Also, in some rural areas where East Indians were a majority, there were reported incidents of East Indian attacks on Blacks.

After the election, the Chief questioned the British

governor's fairnesss in the allocation of senate seats to his party and launched an angry attack on the British at a public political meeting at the Georgetown, Parade Ground. As he hinted ominously at the possibility of race war between Africans and East Indians, I saw Steven Osbourne's face tighten. He had gone to the meeting with Belinda, Michael and me, and I sensed that the Chief's remarks had made him think of his relationship with Drupattie. She did not come with us because we felt she might encounter some danger in the angry, political mood prevailing there. In any event, her father, Ragunandan, would not have approved of her attending this meeting because his political allegiance lay with the ruling East Indian party. Moreover, he now seemed less than cordial to his African-Guianese customers with whom he had often shared many a bottle of *Banks* beer over the shop counter on a sweltering tropical afternoon.

As the Chief spoke, alternately shifting from the cultivated eloquence of ruling class London speech to the familiar Creolese dialect, the crowd intermittently roared its approval. While many of his subsequent actions were an attempt to weaken British colonial influence as exerted by the governor, they were more essentially aimed at undermining the power of the democratically elected ruling East Indian majority. Following the meeting at the Parade Ground, the Chief's opposition party passed a resolution demanding the governor's recall because of his refusal to reconsider the matter of the senate seat allocation. He and his political colleagues then squatted in front of the *Public Buildings* in Georgetown to prevent the governor's entry on the day of the formal opening of the new legislature.

Some weeks later, the opposition denounced the East Indian premier's controversial proposed budget as anti-working class and communistic, a contradiction that few cared to debate in an atmosphere of racism and politically fuelled fear of communism. Protests in the largely African-populated capital grew, until finally, in the early afternoon of February 16, 1962, demonstrators, roving bands of hooligans, idlers, and just ordinary folk looted and set fire to large areas of the city's commercial district, much of which was controlled by East Indian businessmen. According to reports, Blacks were attacking East Indians in the capital.

Several looters, loaded with what booty they managed to steal and carry, slowly pedaled their creaking bicycles up Lamaha Street on their way from Georgetown, their faces stained with soot and streaked with sweat. Some donkey carts and horse-drawn dray carts passed along the street, overloaded with items ranging from furniture and electrical appliances to *Bata yachtings*. Motorists, including Leon, the bus driver, who drove a taxi part-time, made several trips to and from Georgetown, their cars laden with stolen goods. The country's security forces seemed unable or unwilling to contain the lawlessness.

At one point, Leon stopped at our gate to ask my mother, "Nursie, you want anything? Man, Ah manage to get some nice bolts uh cloth from Jaigobin Dry Goods on Water Street. Pick wha' you want."

With his usual generosity, he added, "Fuh you, some is free. Beautiful material, man—*peau de soie* and chiffon. Beautiful material. Beautiful material."

Strangely, the riots seemed to have enhanced his familiarity with women's dress material. My mother stuck her head out the living room window. When he saw her look of disapproval, his tone changed from expansive generosity to justification.

"Nursie. Nursie, man. If I din tek it somebody else might a' di tek it, an' if dey din tek it, it would a bun up in de store when deh set de fire. Suh is na bess somebody get hol' uh de t'ing? Man, yuh should see *Jargetung*. Is like people gone crazy. Water Street bun too bad. A lef' somebody waitin' fuh me dung by Stabroek Market, suh hustle up if you want anyt'ing. Hustle up! Hustle up!"

I remembered the evening on Regent Street several years before, when his impatience forced my mother into a decision that bore us away from my grandfather. It was then twilight, about this same time of the day. A small crowd, including Joe-Joe and Winston, was gathering around his taxi like carrion crows around an animal carcass in the savannah. Though my mother was a strong supporter of the Chief, she took a stern view of looting and pillage.

"Look, you Mr. Man! Get away from mi' gate!"

"Mr. Man" was the term she reserved for male scoundrels. Bernard heard this and sniggered loudly.

Leon sucked his teeth, muttered something nasty under his breath, turned on his heel and "hustled" away to move his taxi and its contents out of danger's way.

"But Mama," I protested, thinking about her often telling me she could not afford it when I asked for a new dress. "Dat chiffon may make a nice dress fuh me fuh de *LCP* fair. Afta rall, is not like we woulda bin t'iefin' it. I shore if 'Gatha get a hol' uh it, she could—"

"Look, Miss Lady, (I had become the female accomplice of 'Mr. Man.') don't annoy me! You ever hear 'bout a t'ing call 'receivin' stolen goods?' Is jus' as big a crime as t'iefin'. You t'ink I want police runnin' up an' dung mi' front steps? A nevuh see de inside of a jail, an' A doan inten' to!"

My mother's knowledge of the law had been honed by careful reading of the *Chronicle's* "Around the Courts" column and by paying attention to proceedings in cases that preceded 'Gatha's, as they both waited in court during the days when 'Gatha took Eustace there for child support.

My mother's voice took on a pensive tone, and she continued. "You tellin' me 'bout chiffon dress, an' yuh country goin' dung de drain. Mark my words. All uh we gun pay fuh de destruction dat takin' place hay today. All uh we! An' we gun pay fuh years to come. You mark my words!"

"My God," she added as an afterthought. "Deh even bun Booker's."

'Gatha managed to secure a new sewing machine during this crisis. I say "secure" because the sewing machine made its mysterious appearance in the immediate wake of the riots, and thereafter, no one, not even my mother who was adept at getting some of the most closely guarded information out of her, was sure whether 'Gatha had really bought the machine or whether it had "fallen off" a looter's truck. It appeared that 'Gatha took to heart the lessons that she learned from Eustace about life in the lock-ups and kept a judicious silence.

In the west, huge columns of black smoke billowed up from the city all evening and into the next day. To quell the distubances, the British government quickly despatched to the colony troops from a regiment with the ironic, ominous name of the Black Watch, but the racial struggle for our country's troubled political soul had only just begun.

CHAPTER 19

In the period immediately following the events of that Friday, February 16, 1962, race relations in British Guiana became increasingly volatile. Generally, Blacks and East Indians went about their daily business, the men of each race warily eyeing each other as well as the impassive alabaster troops of the Black Watch regiment. Stories began to circulate about the troops. One concerned a British soldier who, sweating profusely in the unfamiliar heat and humidity, went into Mr. Jacobs' cake shop and bought a glass of the local, bitter-tasting non-alcoholic mauby.

"I say, how much of this stuff do you have to drink to get drunk?" he had asked Mr. Jacobs, after taking several swigs.

Amused at the troops' ignorance about the local beverage, the hangers-on sniggered. However, they took serious umbrage with some village women who granted the troops sexual favors. With the fury of men scorned, they branded such women "whores." Many of the young British troops were said to "have an appetite for" local women, and the white soldiers who hung around places like the Blue Lantern in Tiger Bay were reported to be very generous with the eager, bright-eyed women they encircled in the tavern doorway's yawning blue glare and blare.

Ragunandan took a dim view of the riot, especially the toll that it exerted on East Indian businesses in the city. A cold, dead stare now replaced the warm, friendly light in his eyes whenever he dealt with his Black customers, and the days of "overs," little extras that he sometimes added to the goods he sold them, were no more.

Drupattie and I continued to be friends, but riding our bicycles together to and from school became increasingly more unsettling. Whereas formerly, Joe-Joe and Winston would merely taunt us to amuse themselves fleetingly, they now seemed to take us more seriously, and there was a poignant menace in their remarks that simmered with sexual and racial violence, especially to Drupattie. Drupattie and I had never discussed the issue of race, pirouetting skillfully around it to topics that we were more comfortable with. At sixteen, we dealt with the situation in the only way that we could: In silent agreement, we stopped riding to and from school together, speaking to each other mostly in school, where the events that were taking place in the country seemed to cause scarcely a ripple. In English classes, we remained closeted in the stuffy English drawing rooms of Jane Austen's *Pride and Prejudice* and continued to be engaged with Mr. and Mrs. Bennet in the pursuit of proper matrimonial matches for their daughters. We continued to be superficially amused by the antics of Bottom and Quince in *A Midsummer Night's Dream,* and via Miss Burgess' conversational Latin, we still followed Caesar in his relentless drive to dominate Britain.

Mrs. Jordan, the French mistress, despaired over our carelessness in oral comprehension: "I ask you, *Quel temps fait-il?* and you dare to reply, *Il est une heure?*" One day, in the geography class, while I absent-mindedly let my thoughts drift towards what it would be like to live in a Mediterranean climate (Miss Goddard, the geography mistress, had drilled it into us that it was characterized by warm, wet winters; cool, dry summers; and plenty of sunshine all year round), we heard the sounds of shrieks and running footsteps in the corridor outside the geography room. Miss Goddard looked faintly irritated, having been interrupted in her interrogation of Claudette Munroe about what kinds of fruit grew best in this climate. Claudette seemed momentarily relieved. She had not been able to get past the answer of "grapes" (which we only saw at Christmas anyway), so the distraction in the corridor was a welcome respite.

Miss Goddard, like Miss Burgess, was Black and had studied for a degree in geography at a university in Great Britain. She was small and moved with a quiet, unobtrusive rubber-soled grace. We never heard her coming when we were screaming at each other and wreaking general havoc in the form-room. She would simply appear at the door and speak in the reprovingly firm, but quiet "been away" accents of educated Georgetown. Now she rose and moved to the door to see what was going on in the corridor. We heard her intake of breath, and then she froze at the door.

Standing facing her was a young, armed, red-faced British soldier. He could not have been more than about twenty-one, not much older than we. He was bare-headed, sweaty and unkempt. He held his gun about waist-high in a firing position and seemed very unsteady on his feet. From my long acquaintance with Mr. Braithwaite's cavortings on Lamaha Street, I knew immediately that the soldier was drunk. Behind him, I could hear screams and see flashes of green as girls ran for cover. Belinda, who was near the door, was the first to move. Like lightning, she shoved Miss Goddard away from the door, slammed it shut, then moved the bolt in place. We heard the dull thud as the door hit the end of the gun barrel. For once, Miss Goddard abandoned her air of quiet refinement.

"Get down, girls! Get down!" She screamed-sobbed. "For God's sake, get down! Get under your desks if possible!"

"And *be quiet!* Just get *down!*" she hissed, as those who

had not seen the soldier began to ask loudly what was going on.

Belinda, Drupattie and I huddled on the floor. Drupattie's palm felt damp in mine as we squeezed each other's hands in fear. My heart boomed in my ears so loudly that I was sure that everyone else in the room must be hearing it. Feeling as if I was about to lose control of my bladder, as I had done in that moment of incontinence in Mr. Davis' scholarship class so many years before, I steeled myself into control. I wondered how painful it would be to die of a bullet wound. God, I prayed, don't let it hurt too much! Outside the window, a north-easter gently stirred the mango tree in the schoolyard. It was one of those gorgeous, calm, tropical days with a high, blue, blue sky that made one sense a divinity and eternity transcending all the promises that sometimes fall so glibly from the lips of clergymen.

In the corridor, we could hear the soldier muttering drunkenly. At times, his voice rose as he hurled senseless utterances. A few times, he banged on the door with the butt of his gun, and then mercifully, when I was sure that my bladder could stand it no longer, we heard the sound of his heavy boots (a sound that many of us were now coming to recognize) tramping down the corridor. We heard the relieved voice of the headmistress outside in the corridor saying to someone that the soldier had left the building and she had called the police. We remained huddled under our desks, shocked and trembling for some minutes, listening gratefully to, and in awe of, the indescribably sweet sounds of our beating hearts.

Many years later, I would come upon Miss Goddard near a side-walk fruit vendor's stand on Rogers Avenue in Brooklyn. Her hair was then thin and silvery, her back bent somewhat under the weight of her approaching seventy-five years. She was still wrapped in the slim, quiet, dignified grace that she had once worn like a young woman's chiffon neglige, a grace that seemed otherworldly in the work-a-day environment of Caribbean immigrant Brooklyn. As we stood in the winter twilight among the trays of oranges and peaches and apples, we spoke of the what-are-you-up-to-now things, not of that day in the long-ago-and-far-away when we crouched in terrified silence, our lives seeming to hang on the whim of a stranger-invader.

Drupattie was now officially "going around" with Steven Osbourne. They grew closer every day. He would wait for her after school at the corner of Carmichael and Middle Streets, and they would ride home together. Sometimes, as they rode along, he would deliberately steer his bicycle near hers so that their shoulders touched; sometimes he would touch her hand on her handlebar as if to make a point. He seemed as intoxicated with her as she was with him. Neither the wagging tongues in the village nor the taunts of Joe-Joe and Winston could cool their passion for each other. Sometimes, they could be seen studying together in the Public Free Library on Main Street. Before the riot fires had consumed the Brown Betty soda fountain, they would sit there, their heads close together. Now they seized every opportunity to be alone together on the seawall or in the promenade or botanic gardens. My mother was sure that this spelt trouble and that if Drupattie did not look out, she would soon "have a bun in de oven," as my mother so descriptively put it with her usual flair for the metaphorical.

My mother also felt that it was only a matter of time before Ragunandan found out and that his new racial attitude would spell either the end of the relationship or of them both. Based on Drupattie's confidences, I can only try to reconstruct what probably transpired between them in those precious stolen moments.

Steven lay beside her on the seawall as the ocean breeze played on them. The sounds of the city were muted by the faraway dull roar of the Atlantic off in that mysterious, beckoning darkness. An occasional mosquito or sandfly flitted playfully between them. They heard the distant sounds of the Guianese popular vocalist, Eddie Hooper, singing "Passing Memories," the local hit of the early sixties, sounds that wafted over to them from a juke box near Fort Groyne under a full, full tropical moon.

Steven wanted them to get married and leave the country right after they had both taken their GCE "A" Levels.

"How can I marry you?" Drupattie asked, her large eyes moving lovingly over his face, her hand playing on his cheek with infinite tenderness. "You know what Pa an' Uncle Gobin t'ink of an East Indian gyurl marryin' a Black fella. An' you really believe Miss Oz would want an Indian daughter-in-law? It would be hard for us in dis country. Hard, hard."

"To hell wid dese people!" Steven replied spiritedly.

"Dey busy messin' up dis country, an' yet dey tryin' to tell us how to run our lives. I love you, Drew. I love you, an' I want us to be where we could shout out an' tell di' worl' dat we love each other an' where di' worl' wun give a damn about whether we from two different races or dat we will have *Dougla* children. One day, di' minds of the people here will change, but we wun live to see it, an' I wun give you up jus' to please dem."

He turned over on his side, facing her fully, and kissing her long and hungrily.

"Steven, today Uncle Gobin told me to tell Pa dat 'e comin' tomorrow to discuss somet'ing important. Is one of two t'ings: Eiduh Uncle Gobin comin' to discuss an arranged marriage for me or he comin' to tell Pa dat he heard somet'ing about you an' me. I could sense it from how 'e look at me. Eiduh way is not good."

"God! I would hate to see you en' up like Balgobin's daughters, Lilowtie an' Chandrowtie. If Balgobin get his way, you wun even get to do medicine, much less marry me. He would have you tied down in a house makin' children and *clappin' roti*. Drew, we may even have to leave before we do di' 'A' Level exams."

Drupattie took a long, pensive look out into the ocean's beckoning roar. "Sometimes A feel like a doan belong to me. Sometimes A t'ink dat A belong to Pa an' to Uncle Gobin an' to you, an' maybe even dat medicine is not what A should be thinkin' of doin'. Afta rall, how many Indian women we know here who study medicine? Sometimes Uncle Gobin make me feel like an ole maid who wastin' mi' time in school."

Steven pulled her close, pressing her tightly to him.

"Drew, you will never be an ole maid as long as we love each other." By then, Eddie Hooper slipped into his other hit, "Where Are Your Friends Now?" and reluctantly, they left the seawall, their arms wrapped around each other. In the distance, the Kitty market clock tolled the hour, and the eerie sound of a jumbie bird—"oohwhoyou"—came to them through the branches of a coconut tree.

Balgobin never got the chance to tell Ragunandan what was on his mind because early the next morning, Ragunandan slipped into a diabetic coma and died in a Booker's taxi on the way to the Public Hospital. His relatives, friends and customers all dropped by to console his wife, Rookmin, and Drupattie. Later, according to Hindu religious custom, Ragunandan's body was cremated on the East Demerara foreshore. Ragunandan had bequeathed all his possessions to Balgobin, and almost before Ragunandan's ashes had even settled, Balgobin arranged for the sale of the shop and its effects and for Rookmin and Drupattie to move into his own household.

CHAPTER 20

1963 marked the end of most of our remaining inno-
cence. Besides being the year of the crippling eighty-day
general strike against the East Indian dentist's government,
it signaled a widespread, frightening acceleration of interracial hostility in British Guiana. In Georgetown, there
were reports of East Indians' being severely beaten by
Blacks. In the rural areas like the Courentyne and West
Demerara coast, one heard that Blacks were violently set
upon by Indians. Belinda, Drupattie and I filled the long
days of the strike studying for the GCE "O" levels. To our
mild dismay, the examination proceded despite the strike,
which caused food and fuel shortages that were beginning
to take hold. Coal pots, formerly used mostly in some rural
cooking, were making their appearance in Kitty and
Georgetown. Some days in the exam room, as we tried to
concentrate on the questions, we could hear above our stomachs' growl the chants of strikers marching along nearby
Main Street, then on into High Street to the Public Buildings. Occasionally, we heard the sounds of gunshots. On
other days, we would hear the amplified yells of an excited
political speaker at the Parade Ground on Middle Street and
the corresponding rallying roar of the crowd. Politics (and
exams) proceeded apace in spite of the British occupation and
the state of emergency. Belinda and I yearned for the end of
the examinations so that we could join the crowds.

Frightened for Drupattie's safety during this period,

Balgobin arrived to pick her up in Leon's taxi. With the bus drivers' having joined the general strike, Leon was then free to devote his full attention to the taxi, which business was, at that time, understandably more lucrative than ever. Balgobin used Leon's services, not because he had any particular desire to patronize a Black man's business, but because, in his fear, he hoped that Leon's presence would deter any hostile Blacks who might want to attack him. Balgobin also felt the fearful need for his own presence in the taxi in order to protect Drupattie from any sexual advances he felt Leon might make toward her. Afta rall, all dese Black man is de same. Wha' dat me hear 'bout she an' Miss Oz son? Ragu mussie de mad! If Ragu din pay de exam fee, she woulda done bin married. Exam, me behine! A wha' young gyal want wid school? Dem is fuh marry mek good wife.

Balgobin continued his anxious ruminations as the taxi turned onto Carmichael Street. Broodingly, he dug himself into his corner of the smelly vehicle. Soon, Harripaul and Ramdat would come and they would talk. A family wid a whole rice mill! Chandrowtie or Lilowtie shoulda bin suh lucky! One day Drupattie will t'ank me!

Two days later, he sold Drupattie's bicycle for thirty dollars.

Miss Ida had made Balgobin and Miss Oz aware of her suspicions concerning Steven and Drupattie's relationship. On a few evenings, as Miss Ida made her way from Bible class meetings at church, she had seen them riding home together from the seawall. At first, she could not believe her eyes. Afta rall, she reasoned, Miss Oz would never allow her son to keep company wid a coolie gyurl, an' everybody know how racial Balgobin was. Mi' Lord, he would nevva allow such a t'ing.

Still, she resolved to keep a sharp lookout in case she saw the couple again. Her chance came on another evening as she was hurrying home to help Miss Ada with a wedding order for cook-up rice. Drupattie and Steven rode past her, holding hands and giggling intimately. Miss Ida heard their voices and clearly saw their outlines as they passed under the street lamp's glare where Shirley's body had lain.

Miss Oz was cooking breakfast on an old Dover stove in the kitchen. The smell of woodsmoke and *pepperpot* filled the air. Sweat poured from her plump, round, shiny face as she adjusted her husband's old felt hat on her head, poked at the fire, and then stirred the dark contents of the large iron pot. By midday, Mr. Osbourne would be home and the children, including Steven, would also be arriving for breakfast. Most people went home for breakfast and a brief rest before going back to their jobs or to school.

The warm kitchen, occasionally touched by the flitting Demerara breeze, was usually quite comforting to Miss Oz as she did her housework. When she could spare it, she took time off during the morning, sucking her teeth as she brushed away the annoying flies that were attracted by the dried fruits she was grinding to set aside in rum for Christmas black cake. Tenderly nursing a warm enamel cup of *Ovaltine*, she lumbered slowly into the sitting room and carefully placed the cup on the coffee table. She then pushed open and propped up a few more Demerara windows in the gallery, sighed deeply, and settled her large posterior into the comfortable Berbice chair that creaked protestingly. Her eyes blissfully half-closed, she followed the fortunes of the radio soap opera heroine, Portia, in the serial, *Portia Faces Life*, set in some foreign, and to Miss Oz, decidedly more advantageous, female environment than her own. It was sheer bliss, almost equivalent to the religious ecstasy she experienced every Sunday at Miss Ida's church. Thus, she gratefully found refuge from the hard, unrelenting drudgery of her life—just as her husband did in the glasses of *Russian Bear* rum that consumed his fear.

Anointed by reflections on Portia's experience and buoyed to face the tedium of her chores, Miss Oz would later return to the kitchen. By breakfast time, as Mr. Osbourne and the children ate, she was glued to the *Bush* radio for the serial, *A Man Called Shepherd*, and after the others returned to work and school, she was lulled by the hum of the tune, "Beautiful Dreamer" that introduced another radio soap opera, *A Second Spring*. The seductive, mellow voice of the male announcer would intone the questions so many of the village women knew by heart and perhaps silently asked themselves: *"Can a woman who has once loved completely ever find... true love again? Can she find.... a second spring?"* Miss Oz mouthed the words with the announcer. Then she immersed herself in the endless serial misfortunes of the fictional lovers, Christine Harding and Wade Morgan. Often, she and my mother earnestly conjectured at some length as to whether the Harding-Morgan nuptials, beset with recurrent obstacles, would ever be realized.

Fridays were a particularly anxious time for Miss Oz because by three o'clock, she had to be at her husband's workplace to secure her share of Mr. Osbourne's paypacket before any of the "bad 'omen" who hung around the wharf area on payday managed to lure him to the seedy "short-time" rooming houses in the city—or before any of his workmates dragged him off to binge in the city taverns.

Leon, the bus/taxi driver, was sensitive to the importance of Miss Oz's weekly mission, and when he rolled by her stop at half-past-two on Fridays, he would be looking out for her. If she were not there, he would send a "small boy" to run quick, run guh call Miss Oz, while the other passengers sucked their teeth and writhed impatiently.

Slowly, the "small boy" would walk a few feet from the

bus and yell deafeningly, **"Miss Oz! Miss Oz! Miss Oz! Come quick! Come quick! Bus come!"**

Miss Oz would bustle out, sweating profusely, her bare neck liberally splashed with *Mennen's* talcum powder, her seersucker dress clinging to her large thighs. She would thank Leon repeatedly, glancing apologetically at the irate passengers on the Kitty-Regent bus. By Friday evening, exhausted by her foray into the rough-and-tumble world of her husband's work environment, she would return home alone and allow herself to be soothed into forgetfulness by the radio soap opera, *Aunt Mary*, billed as "a *human* story... about *real* people."

Miss Ida settled herself into a chair at the kitchen table opposite Miss Oz. Miss Ida's presence that Friday morning grated on Miss Oz since it interfered with the latter's reflections on the domestic happenings of the week past and with her household planning for that to come. She knew that Ida was a repository of intimate titbits about the village people's private lives, and she sensed that Ida had something important to relate that pertained directly to her own situation. Miss Oz was also aware that, as much as she detested Miss Ida's snooping, much of her general information would prove to be fairly accurate. Anyone with a drop of sense knew it was foolhardy to ignore a warning from Miss Ida based on what she professed to know. Miss Oz, therefore, regretfully put aside thoughts of the *Portia* episode of which Miss Ida's presence now deprived her, and assumed the general demeanor of an inviting audience.

"Suh, how yuh do? How dem chirrun, nuh gyurl?" Miss Ida asked Miss Oz, glancing at her briefly out of the corner of her eye.

"Well, whuh Ah gun tell you, gyurl? *Porely an' sof'ly.* Eileen sick home, yuh know. She got visitors from Red

China." Miss Oz quickly added the last sentence so as to keep Ida from jumping to the wrong conclusion.   "Cora tryin' at *Tutorial*, an' A hopin' dat Teacher Davis put de fear uh de Lord in F'edrick suh 'e *kyan* pass de scholarship. You remember how Teacher Davis de wuk wonders wid Steven?"

Miss Oz sensed that Steven was going to be the main subject of discussion, and to make it easy for Miss Ida, she deliberately steered the conversation in his direction. This interaction between the two women was like a delicately choreographed dance, the steps of which they both instinctively knew.

Lately, Miss Oz had begun to sense a gulf developing between her and her eldest child.   Almost overnight, it seemed, he had been transformed from a "small boy" in short pants into a tall, gangling, young man, who was the opening bowler on the boys' college cricket team and a student with the self-confidence to challenge his teachers' opinions and criticize the politicians.

Me Lord?   'E even had de *idocity* to say dat we Black people was jus' as guilty as de Eas' Indians in de trouble we havin'!

Imagine dat!   Coolie people who everybody know would stir up trouble before you could say "Jack Robinson!" Only las' week de chile tellin' me dat de white people confuse Black people wid to much religion, dat while deh givin' we paradise in de hereafter, deh tekin' we birt'right hey on eart'.   Imagine de sacrilege! Well, I had to tell 'e, "not under my roof!"   'E t'ink 'e get suh big dat I wun cut 'e tail, but 'e would be surprise!

Miss Ida stepped quickly into the opening that Miss Oz had just given her.

"Eh! Eh!" said Miss Ida, as though she had only just remembered something. "Eh! Eh! Ah see Steven las' night."

Miss Oz sensed that there was more to follow.

"Oh so? Wheh yuh see 'e?"

"Yuh shun only ass me wheh ah see 'e. Yuh should ass me *who* ah see 'e *wid*," said Miss Ida, pursing her lips and looking directly at Miss Oz for the first time since her arrival.

"Awright. Who yuh see 'e wid?"

Miss Ida paused for dramatic effect. "Well, he an' Ragunandan daughter been ridin' dung from de seawall las' night. An' mine you! Is not de firs' time ah see dem! Deh was actually holdin' han's. It look like you got Cary Grant on you han's, man."

She added this last bit with a faint hint of derision.

Miss Oz did not mind if Steven's compassion for East Indians destroyed what she termed his "good judgment" about them. She was not even so troubled about his distaste for religion. Lord knows, in a way 'e was right. De English minister dung at St. James-de-Less always talkin' but forgivin' yuh enemies an' turnin de odda cheek while 'e emptyin' yuh back pocket into de collection plate. But the matter of Steven's affair with an East Indian girl was cause for fear and concern. There would be hell to pay when Mr. Osbourne got home. She would make sure of that. She would *progue* 'e an' progue 'e like he was a bad tooth; she would cry piteously; Mr. Osbourne would be forced to do something. To t'ink dat Steven riskin' 'e neck wid de people gyurl chile. An' ev'rybody know how dem people like chop up wid cutlass. De boy mus' be a jackass! An' at a time like dis to! When deh got all dis strike an' race riot in de country! Doan worry wid Steven! Ole people seh *"sof'ly, sof'ly, ketch monkey"* an' 'e gun soon learn de meanin' uh dat!

Miss Ida got up to leave, behaving as though she had suddenly remembered a chore she had to do.

"Well, blessings upon you, Miss Oz," she said, sanctimoniously, as she made for the door. From inside the bedroom, the Simmons bed creaked. Eileen Osbourne, who would later tell Drupattie about this exchange, turned over and coughed.

CHAPTER 21

Ramdat Seelochan sat uneasily in Balgobin's little parlour. He and his father, Harripaul, were visiting Balgobin on serious business. Harripaul was the prosperous owner of a rice mill on the Courentyne, and he expected that Ramdat would soon take over the major portion of the operation. There was just one matter left to be addressed before Ramdat, his last child and only son, assumed almost total control since Harripaul had already suffered a nearly crippling stroke. At twenty-four, Ramdat had still not chosen a bride, engrossed as he was in helping his father run the rice milling business. For a young man who had left school in fifth standard at the age of fourteen, Ramdat had not done so badly, Harripaul thought. If Harripaul became further incapacitated, Ramdat could easily carry on. Yet, there was one thing missing. Ramdat needed a wife. Afta rall, Harri thought, a man mus' have sons to kerry on 'e name an' mek de business prospa even mo'.

Harripaul knew that his good friend Balgobin had a niece (nice lookin' gyal to) who was just the right age. True, she had had some schooling, an' ev'rybody know dat fuh gyal pickney, "lil learnin' is a dangerous t'ing." But Ramdat would tek she in han' and *bruk* she in. By de time dey get she to de Courentyne, Ramdat mother, Dookie, would mek she see straight.

Ramdat used the fingernail of his little finger in an effort to extract a piece of curried mutton that had become stuck between his back teeth. Simultaneously, he made short, nervous thip-thip-thipping noises as he tried to pry the bit of food loose with the tip of his tongue. He had to concede that even though he was angered and dismayed by the sullen, contemptuous look Drupattie had cast in his direction when she had first seen him, he was heartened by the fact that her mother, Rookmin, and Balgobin's wife, Surojinie, were excellent cooks. Obviously, they would have trained Drupattie in this, one of the most important of all domestic requirements. Surojinie and Rookmin had laid out a delicious meal of *dholl*, rice, roti, curried mutton and *bajie* for him and Harripaul, who had belched appreciatively at the end. Ramdat was sure that, in time, Drupattie would forget about the city with its educational and other entice- ments and that she would settle down to become a quiet, obedient, dutiful Hindu wife and mother. She would have strong sons, all like him, with a head for the business. Balgobin, Harripaul and he had had a good laugh over the idea of her wanting to become a doctor. Imagine dat! Afta rall, doctorin' was fuh men.

Ramdat's own cousin, Mahesh, was studyin' dat now in de United States and would soon send for his younger brother, Ramesh, who also wanted to study medicine.

For all his nervousness, Ramdat had to fight the feeling of lassitude that was closing over him on this hot, rather stifling Sunday afternoon. He was dark and very slight looking with a sliver of a moustache that pulled down the corners of his lips and lent a hint of cruelty and meanness to his thin lips. From its stand in the sitting room, the *Bush* radio blared forth the sounds of East Indian music as the popular Indian female singer, Lata Mangeshkar, her voice gliding silkily across the suffocating heat, took over smoothly from lyrics of the male vocalists, Mukesh and Rafi. From the wall, Lakshmi, the Hindu goddess of good- ness and light, looked benignly yet somewhat indifferently down on the three men. Balgobin, who had settled comfortably into the hammock that hung in a corner of the room, declared, "De yoke of an egg would burs' me" and made contented clicking noises with his tongue as he got down to the business of clearing food from his teeth. Then he cleared his throat in preparation for the negotiations that would soon take place. He calmly brushed away a fly that had begun to crawl on his face as though it was feverishly searching for some explanation of his impending actions.

The only other sounds came from the kitchen, where the women clanged pots and pans and enamel plates as they washed them and talked in tense, whispered tones.

Drupattie wore an old white school blouse, stained bright red in front with magenta from the East Indian *Pagwah* festival that March. When Balgobin sold her bicycle, she knew this action marked the first phase in the loss of her freedom. I imagine that, standing in Surojinie's hot, still unfamiliar kitchen as unfamiliar men negotiated her future, she realized that education had still left her hopelessly and tragically ill-equipped for situations such as these. How did a young Hindu woman in mid-sixties British Guiana cope with her uncle's rage over her romance with a young Black man? Someone had mentioned the affair to Balgobin in the course of his milk rounds, and he had come very near beating her. Balgobin swore that he would castrate Steven if he ever heard a whisper of her seeing him again, and Balgobin had quickly contacted Harripaul to start arrangements for her wedding to Ramdat. Balgobin knew there was little chance that Harripaul and Ramdat had heard any rumours of the affair, since they lived far away on the Courentyne. Drupattie wondered how she could make him see that her gender did not preclude her potential to become a good doctor some day; that race was irrelevant in matters of the heart; that Ramdat's marriage ring would slowly strangle her. Ramdat, who regarded a woman almost as he did his uncle's cows, saw her as a breeding machine. Ramdat, who had the annoying habit of picking his teeth and making clicking noises after meals. Ramdat, whose conversation was limited largely to the details of running the rice mill. She shuddered as a vision flashed before her of herself and Ramdat engaged in sexual intercourse. Oh God, not that! she thought. Then the memory of Steven's hands, gentle on her breasts, reaching over and into her secret places, crossed her mind, and she thought she would go mad.

Also, her mother, Rookmin, though exhausted by her own grief, destitution, and Balgobin's domination, was coming around to the belief that Drupattie should marry a "nice Hindu boy." Afta rall, Rookmin had reasoned to her, at least she (Drupattie) would be mistress of her own house, the wife of a prosperous rice miller, the mother of Hindu sons. How much East Indian gyal wooden give deh eye teet' for such a chance? Eventually, perhaps, she (Rookmin) might even be able to go and live with Drupattie on the Courentyne (also a secret hope of Surojinie and Balgobin) and so escape the curse of being a poor woman in another woman's household. Since yuh fadduh dead, t'ings en' been easy, an' if yuh have feelin's fuh me as yuh mudduh, yuh would lissen to Uncle Bal. Lately Surojinie (whom Rookmin now sarcastically referred to behind her back as "de maddom") had begun to "throw remarks" in their direction, referring to them as *poe great but han' to mout'*. Surojinie had made a great show of being scandalized by Drupattie's relationship with Steven and insisted privately to her husband, Balgobin, dat she wanted de lil whore out de house quick-quick.

Drupattie had protested to Rookmin that when the results of the G.C.E. exam were announced, she was sure she would do well. She would then be qualified for a job in the Civil Service, and she and Rookmin could move to the city.

All this was hard for Rookmin to absorb. She had come

of age at a time when East Indians generally did not work in the Civil Service partly because the colonial government, the major employer, had then required that government employees be Christian. Rookmin recalled that some East Indians took Christian first names and even Anglicized their surnames in an effort to reap the opportunities offered by the colonial government. Others, like Ramdat, Harripaul, and Balgobin, clung steadfastly to their culture, pursuing agricultural or individual commercial ventures in order to make a living. Moreover, Rookmin saw no need for a Hindu woman to work in the government service when there was a Hindu man willing to offer her respectability and comfort in marriage. True enough, when Ragu was alive he had encouraged Drupattie wid dis foolishness about bein' independent an' goin' away an' studyin', but Ragu wasn' dere now, an' dey would have to mek do. In fac', dey would have to cut an' contrive.

At this time, too, the country was in the grip of a general strike that had fairly paralyzed the economy. Where would Drupattie find work? As it was, the strike had affected food supplies, transportation and other important areas of Government functioning. A political solution seemed very distant at best, since the country appeared to be on the brink of a race war. In normal circumstances, Rookmin and Drupattie would have suffered considerable hardship. As it was, their situation grew more intolerable each day. Drupattie felt a noose tightening around her future.

That afternoon, the men parted with satisfied smiles. Drupattie went into the little bedroom she shared with her mother and two of Balgobin's younger children and wrote a letter that she handed to me the next day.

"Give dis to Steven," she said, quietly. Then she told me all that I have just related. "You're not really goin' to marry dat Ramdat, Drew?" I half-asked, half-said, half-laughed in disbelief.

"Uncle Bal said dat if I don't, he *kyan* fine people to kill Steven. You know, at a time like dis in de country, it is easy to get away wid murder. Uncle Bal could make it look like a racial attack, an' 'e know people who could do it."

She shuddered slightly. A cock crowed in the early morning silence; another answered and another answered that one.

It was the hot August holidays, and we were sitting on a bench under a mango tree in my backyard. A kiskadee bird went "Kiss-ka-dee, kiss-kiss-ka-dee" in the distance. Already, the day had started warm and dry, a precursor to the smothering heat that would develop later. My mother and Bernard had not yet awakened, but I knew the rhythm of Drupattie's soft taps on the door, a sound I had grown accustomed to since the time of our winning the scholarships together, time that now seemed an eternity ago. We were then twelve, when romance came in small, handy, sixty-four page English comics and *True Confessions* and *Tan* magazines that we read and re-read in secret and giggled over, in which there were always happy endings. We were now seventeen, and love had left the pages, entered our experience and declared itself serious business.

"Doan give in, Drew! Fight them!" I urged. Easy for me to say.

"I kyant go up agains' all uh dem," she said, frowning and shrugging her shoulders in bleak resignation.

It was like visiting a critically ill, close relative in hospital and hearing the doctors say that they were very sorry but that they had done everything they could. I suddenly realized that for all we had shared, I never really understood her world. Choking with tears, her shoulders drooping, she got up and turned away from me.

The next day, a dust-covered *Vauxhall Velox* Berbice hire car pulled up at Balgobin's *gyap*. Ramdat and Harripaul got out; Ramdat leaned into the driver's window and told the apparently impatient driver to "wait ya. A-we a come back jis-jis now."

Balgobin came down his front steps and met them with three large, battered, brown suitcases, the same ones that Drupattie and Rookmin had taken with them when they went to live with Balgobin after Ragunandan's death. The two women, both dressed in colorful gauzy saris, emerged onto the landing at the top of the rickety stairs.

Balgobin had neatly killed two birds with one stone. He succeeded in throwing Rookmin into the matrimonial settlement that he had negotiated with Ramdat and Harripaul. Therefore, she would live with the couple on the Courentyne. The sole inheritor of Ragunandan's business, Balgobin had now unburdened himself of the financial responsibility for his brother's widow and orphan. He placed the suitcases at Ramdat's feet and breathed a long sigh of relief.

Unusually dressed in her sari, her eyes modestly cast down, Drupattie now exuded that very delicate, alabaster, almost ethereal beauty that one saw in the faces of East Indian actresses in billboard pictures along the East Coast Public Road; the statue of the Blessed Virgin in the Catholic Church on David Street; or the Christmastime dolls in Fogarty's show window. She was stunningly unfamiliar to me. Ramdat ushered the two women and Harripaul into the back seat of the taxi and sat in front next to the driver. Balgobin, Surojinie and the children waved goodbye from the front gate, and the car took off with what sounded like an animal wail of pain.

Both women were gone, vanished into a vortex of matrimony on the Courentyne.

I never saw or heard from Drupattie again.

CHAPTER 22

For days after I had given it to him, I wondered vaguely about the contents of Drupattie's letter to Steven. It would be thirty years before I would know, and by then she would be nothing more to Steven and me than a shadow of memory. He received the letter from me with a look of slight puzzlement but quiet apprehension, putting it away in his pocket to read later. He must have known that Drupattie was being subjected to intense pressure to end the relationship.

Miss Oz kept my mother abreast of her own efforts in this direction. She herself had approached Balgobin at her gate early one morning when he was delivering milk. Having awakened before anyone else in the house, Miss Oz had lumbered down the steps as quickly and as quietly as her large size permitted, sucking her teeth softly as she took care to avoid a creaky treader that, for years, Mr.Osbourne had been promising to repair.

In whispered, urgent tones, Miss Oz had told Balgobin what she knew. They both agreed that East Indians and Blacks were really not supposed to be together in a romantic way. Afta rall, it does bring *suh* much trouble. They reflected on the fact that they had lived together as neighbors for many years and that people of both races had always known how to behave and sensed what was appropriate and what was not. She assured him that Steven's behaviour made her "shame shame," that she would see what she could do, but that he (Balgobin) also needed to control Drupattie before *boat go a falls*.

However, her auditory perceptions, sharpened by years of radio soap opera addiction, startled her into an awareness of Balgobin's contempt for her son evident in his tone when he asked, "Suh how lang now dis boy a meet dis gyal?" Miss Oz could not see Balgobin's face clearly in the semi-dark, but she was sure that a disturbing menace had crept into his expression. Some protective maternal instinct whispered a warning to her in the Demerara semi-darkness, and she abruptly ended the conversation and tip-toed back up the stairs, forgetting to avoid the creaking treader. Balgobin got back on his bicycle, his metal cans clanking loudly, his curses increasing in frequency and force as the stray dogs resumed their pursuit.

In keeping with her vow to "progue 'e an' progue 'e like a bad tooth" over Steven's affair with Drupattie, Miss Oz had solicited Mr. Osbourne's support.

Irritatingly, however, he remained unmoved.

"Look Gladys," he had responded. "De boy got to sow 'e oats. Yuh behavin' like dis is de fus woman dat 'e gun evuh deh wid. Man, gi' de boy a res'. You remembuh how much 'oman I had before you?"

"An' how much yuh *still* got!" she exclaimed, irritably.

He was a frequent "Blue Lantern" and "Red Light Bar" patron, and she knew that he had recurrent affairs with the women who hung around these taverns. One day in the Kitty market, one of them had even had the nerve to "cut her eyes" and "throw a remark" at Miss Oz!

Finally, Miss Oz was greatly relieved to hear that Balgobin had (as she dramatically put it) "spirited Drupattie off" to the Courentyne to be married.

On a hot early Sunday afternoon very much like the one on which Ramdat and Harripaul had visited Balgobin, Miss Oz sat in my mother's kitchen, fanning herself with a locally made straw fan, the soft underflesh of her large upper forearm swinging gently with her movements, and sweat pouring from her brow. It was a few days after Drupattie's departure. Sighing heavily, Miss Oz propped her elbows on the kitchen table.

"An' de brazen lil miss even had de nerve to write 'e a farewell letter! A fine it de odda day when A was cleanin' out 'e dresser draw. Once dese coolie gyurls get deh hooks in a Black boy, is blessed hell to pry dem loose. At one time, A was even t'inkin' dat a mighta de had to go an see Mama Rose to fix t'ings up."

Miss Oz sighed heavily.

In addition to having a reputation for bringing reluctant, apprehensive male suitors to the wedding altar, the obeah woman, Mama Rose, was known to be able to end unpalatable relationships for her clients. Miss Oz had once contacted Mama Rose about a young woman from the Blue Lantern vicinity who had a particularly tenacious grip on Mr. Osbourne's affections. After Miss Oz's visit to Mama Rose, during which she left the obeah woman with an earring (not her own) that she had found in Mr. Osbourne's pocket, the young woman in question had not only developed some serious, medically unfathomable illness but had begun to lose weight dramatically. Mr. Osboure who always professed to like *t'ick* women, "women wid good, good size," had slowly seemed to lose interest and moved on. My mother had steupsed her teeth when she reflected on Mama Rose's "success" with this "case" since my mother knew that the young woman had been a sickle cell outpatient at the hospital well before she had ever been subjected to the obeah woman's "attentions." In any event, the rumour persisted in the village spit press that the young woman's illness was a result of the fact that "Mama Rose do she," and the villagers remained suitably and dutifully awed by her alleged supernatural powers.

The pot of blackeye pea soup bubbled happily on the stove, making the kitchen hotter than usual. My mother had gone to a special service at St. George's Cathedral in the city, had been heating up a late lunch and had added some water to the pot when she heard the gate creak and saw Miss Oz coming in. She had taken out her "good" bowls into which she would ladle soup that they would eat while they talked. She tumbled cassavas, eddoes and yams into the soup bowls with a splash.

"I spen' a lot uh time an' effort on Steven, an' I en' do it fuh han' 'e ovuh to dem people in de en'. When de time come, Steven gun marry a nice Black gyurl an' dat is dat."

In response to this, my mother had murmured something noncommittal and unintelligible as she ladled the soup. Her own objection to Drupattie and Steven's relationship evolved from the danger in which it placed them both, not from any antipathy to interracial relationships. Besides, since she was my friend, Drupattie evoked the same maternal concern from her that Gwennie Braithwaite and Belinda had. Privately to me, my mother had expressed the view that Miss Oz sometimes tended to *overdo de do* and that she had the dangerous proclivity to "try to force God han'," an action against which my mother had admonished me when as a child, I had tried to reunite her with her father.

We now hardly saw Steven. He seemed to have withdrawn into himself. He came and went, gave us a "hi" and "right" and moved on. Once the most voluble member of our group, he became the sole, listless inhabitant of his own silent city of sorrow.

He now studied and played cricket with an almost solitary intensity. His name had been tossed around as one of those likely to win the prestigious Guiana Scholarship that would enable him to follow in the footsteps of many of the colony's best and brightest, like Miss Burgess. It was expected that like them, he would embark for one of England's finest universities and return to the colony to join the privileged Black professional middle class.

As far as Miss Oz was concerned, Steven would get over the separation from Drupattie. Now she could get back to the tranquilizing world of radio make-believe, secure in the knowledge that Drupattie's marriage signalled the end of her anxiety—or so she thought.

CHAPTER 23

By the time Drupattie was married to Ramdat, the eighty-day general strike was over. However, racial animosity between Blacks and East Indians raged on in the country areas and the city. One night in early November, just as the tune "Beautiful Dreamer" was announcing the radio soap opera, *A Second Spring*, news spread down Lamaha Street of a commotion in Miss Oz's house.

Steven had been riding through Thomas Lands in the twilight after a school cricket match when he was accosted by four East Indian men armed with sticks. They pulled him off his bicycle and started to beat and kick him. Some blows landed about his head, and he screamed in fear, pain and surprise. Luckily for him (for Thomas Lands was a non-residential area that was usually quite deserted at this time), Police Superintendent Nelson Irving (he of the investigation of Shirley's murder), Justice Day (whose car Bernard had damaged when we were younger) and one other man had just left the golf house and were driving along Thomas Road when they came upon the beating in progress.

Colonial expatriates frequently congregated over gin and tonic or rum and ginger at the Thomas Lands golf house. (Few local people knew how to play golf, and their association with the golf course was often only by way of their being service workers).

Police Superintendent Nelson Irving had been trained at the British Royal Police Academy, and even though local people of African and East Indian descent felt that he had slight respect for them, he was a great believer in the necessity for law, order and fairness. He immediately had Justice Day stop the car, drew his gun, which he always carried with him these days, emerged and fired into the air. The four assailants fled across a nearby bridge into the twilight of Thomas Lands, leaving a battered, bleeding and half-conscious Steven lying by the roadside.

Soon after Irving and the other two men had Steven admitted to the Public Hospital, word of the incident reached Miss Oz even though she had no telephone. A hospital maid, who was Mr. Osbourne's cousin, was present at the Casualty Department when Steven was admitted, and she related the incident to a taxi driver who was parked outside the hospital. The taxi driver, who had once worked with Mr. Osbourne on the wharf, took a fare down to the Stabroek Market, where he conveyed the news to Leon, the bus driver, at the Stabroek bus terminus; on his return trip from Stabroek to Kitty on the Kitty-Regent, Leon stopped outside Miss Oz's house, leaving his passengers fuming in the bus, while he ran in and told her that Steven had been beaten to death by eight East Indian men. Many Black people in the neighborhood were furious over the incident. By the time that Leon's information was corrected, it was too late. Black people who knew the Osbournes simmered with hostility over the incident.

Two of his East Indian co-workers on the wharf had warned Mr. Osbourne that Steven should be careful. They knew friends of Balgobin and had heard rumours that Steven had written to Drupattie; that her new husband, Ramdat, had discovered the letter, and that, outraged, he had contacted Balgobin. Even though Mr. Osbourne and Miss Oz were both aware of Balgobin's bitter distaste for interracial affairs, Drupattie's marriage and Steven's apparent resignation to the course of events had dispelled any apprehension they might have had.

Steven well near lost his life. He suffered a severe concussion and serious internal injuries that caused almost fatal internal bleeding. The police never found the assailants. At a time when racial attacks were becoming so common, the understaffed police force was hard pressed and overworked.

Following his discharge from the hospital, Steven grew even more withdrawn. One peaceful evening in late 1963, as the sun sent its last rays over the coconut and mango tree tops and as many little lights were lit in East Indian homes for the festival of *Diwali*, he and Mr. Osbourne boarded the Kitty-Regent when it stopped outside their house. They carried no luggage, but Steven was dressed more carefully and neatly than usual. He had lost much weight since the incident so that his "good" gaberdine pants seemed to hang a little loosely about his waist. I was reminded of the occasion when, a frail sickly child, he had been forced by Miss Oz to wear her shoes to school—when as a new scholarship boy, he had first left the village to enter the alien culture of the boys' secondary school, and when he had ridden past the silent figures of Joe-Joe, Winston, Fine T'ings and Bruk-Up, perhaps sadly sensing that while he would never again belong to their world, he did not fit (perhaps never would) into the new one for which he was destined either. As frail and defenseless as he seemed then, so in some strange way, he appeared now.

This time Joe-Joe, Winston, Fine T'ings and Bruk-up sat quietly on Mr. Jacob's shop bridge watching him board the bus. Toothpicks dangled from the lips of Joe-Joe and Winston, a cigarette hung carelessly from Bruk-up's. A bird-cage containing a restless little robin lay on the bridge beside Fine T'ings. (He used the bird for gambling bets about its singing). The young men were unusually quiet. A warm wind quietly rustled the leaves of the sapodilla tree in the Osbourne yard as Miss Oz and her daughter, Eileen, stood on the landing of the front steps and saw the men off.

Radio Demerara was devoting an hour that evening to the East Indian festival of *Diwali*. I remember that as the bus pulled away, the instrumental sounds of the haunting East Indian love song, "*Sohani Raat,*" floated liltingly on the north-easter that blew in from the Atlantic. With its enormous popularity among East Indians as well as Blacks, and at a time when there was such ugly hatred between the two groups, the sweet, gentle "*Sohani Raat*" spoke to us all, in a strangely compelling, almost unearthly way, of the human soul's startling potential for amazing grace. Steven and Drupattie had often lain in each other's arms on the seawall and listened to the melody on still, black-velvet Demerara nights, the sound wafting in and out on the sea breeze from the juke-box in a nearby shack.

Diwali was the celebration of the East Indian new year, the triumph of good over evil, the appearance of light in a world darkened by violence, hatred, fear and hopelessness. On that evening of *Diwali,* the festival of lights that he and Drupattie had loved so much, Steven skipped softly out of our circle and across the ocean to England.

One wintry evening thirty years later, as I was gingerly feeling my way along a slippery sidewalk in the icy twilight of Washington, D.C., a graying, well groomed, heavy-set, somewhat middle-aged Black man momentarily lost his footing and bumped into me. I had been working all day in the Library of Congress and was tired and eager to get home. He too was hurrying, and if we had not grabbed hold of each other and done a funny little dance to keep our balance, we would both have fallen to the sidewalk.

"I-I-I'm sorry," he said. "Are you hurt? I should have been paying more attention."

I said no and quickly started to moved on. But something in the sound of his voice, the way he talked, his loping gait, took me back down the corridor of the years to warm sunsets and cool Atlantic breezes. I stopped and turned.

"Steven?" I asked uncertainly. "Steven?" A little louder.

"Yes?" he answered slowly, his tone more of an inquiry than a response.

"Steven Osbourne?"

Slowly, he started to walk back towards me, a look of pure amazement spreading over his face. He called my name with the same stunned disbelief with which I had addressed him.

"Oh my G-God," he stuttered. "Where have you been all these years?"

We hugged long and hard, then embraced so animatedly that we nearly fell again. I felt stinging tears springing to my eyes. We began laughing hysterically, occasionally touching each other on the arm or face as though we each could not believe that the other was real. Over the years, I had infrequently heard his name mentioned in Guyanese circles, that he was doing what everyone said was "important work" with the Commonwealth Secretariat in London, and that occasionally he would visit Washington in a professional capacity, but he had always seemed distant from the tight-knit Guyanese circle in Washington. No one I knew seemed to know precisely what he was doing.

"How have you been?" I asked, animatedly.

"Oh, I've been working with international agencies mostly in London and Washington. Right now, I'm with the Commonwealth Secretariat in an area that focuses primarily on Asian and African countries. When I left home, I went to England, studied law and later got my PhD in International Relations. I've been married... four times. (He added this a little sheepishly). With my kind of job, travelling and all that, marriage can be difficult. What about you?"

There was the faint hint of an English accent in his

words.

"I write and teach," I said. "So far, collectively, I've spent more than half my life in Washington."

He shivered visibly. The temperature was falling.

"We've got to get out of this damned cold. Why don't we have lunch or dinner some time so we can catch up on all we've lost?" he asked.

"Look," he continued, as though something had suddenly occurred to him. "What about meeting me at eight tomorrow night for dinner at the 'Kaieteur'?" He was referring to the popular Guyanese restaurant on Georgia Avenue in the heart of Washington's Black belt.

I agreed to meet him, and we said goodbye, each of us treading gingerly on the slippery sidewalk.

Over dinner at the restaurant, Steven filled in the gaps of his story. Drupattie had written that even though she loved him, existing circumstances forced her to submit to her relatives' wishes. She felt that neither of their families would tolerate their love for each other. As things stood, it was clear that Balgobin was not willing to support her and her mother for much longer, and Drupattie's ability to find work to support them both was severely limited. It would have been culturally unacceptable for her and Steven to live together, and their leaving the country together would have been financially impossible. Apart from Balgobin's obvious objections, there was the added consideration of Miss Oz's resentment, of which Balgobin had made Drupattie aware. The realities of her life dictated that she submit to marriage to Ramdat, she said, but she would always love Steven. Unwilling to cut the lingering ties to him, she had given him her address.

Before Steven could speak to her again, she and Rookmin had left with Ramdat for the Courentyne.

Desperate and unmindful of the danger in which he was placing himself and her, Steven wrote to Drupattie at the address she had given him in her letter. He tried to persuade her to forsake Ramdat and return to him, making wild promises he knew he could not keep.

If she replied, he never got her letters.

The combination of Miss Oz's nagging, Drupattie's departure, the beating and rumours of further threats against his life all weighed heavily on Steven's spirit. After his return from the hospital, Miss Oz had filled him with "builders" like *Ferrol Compound, Marmite,* malt extract, barley soup and barley "tea" in an attempt to help him regain his strength and continue his efforts towards the Guiana Scholarship. But Mr. Osbourne realized that in the interest of his son's safety, they would have to forget about the scholarship. The longer Steven stayed in the colony, the more dangerous his situation (and theirs) became.

Mr. Osbourne knew that a Dutch ship, the *Willemstadt,* was in port Georgetown at the Sandbach Parker wharf and that the Captain had mentioned he needed a stoker, a position which in reality was really that of deckhand. Because of Mr. Osbourne's connections at Sandbach Parker, he was able (in a shorter time than was usual for others) to make arrangements with the agent for Steven to join this ship, "work out" his passage on board, and have the difference paid to him when the ship docked at Southampton where he would disembark. Before reaching Southampton, the ship would make stops at Aruba, Curacao, Bonaire, Barbados, and Funchal in Portugal. The captain held Steven's passport until they reached Southampton. From there, Steven would be on his own. True, he seemed a little frail since the beating, but Mr. Osbourne now felt that work on the ship would restore his stamina, make a man of him, and dissipate any softness gained through bookishness and his association wid dat blasted coolie gyurl.

Mr. Osbourne had had Steven's luggage checked onto the ship the day before so that his departure would not arouse anyone's suspicions. Steven had been headed to board this ship, the *Willemstadt*, when I saw them both leave by bus that *Diwali* afternoon in 1963. Even Miss Oz, usually garrulous about matters related to her children, was now fearful for her remaining family members and tight-lipped about his departure and its circumstances. Later, when Miss Ida inquired, "Eh! Eh! *Is wheh 'e deh?* A doan see Steven nowadays," Miss Oz would say only that he was in England.

Steven told me that, in addition to the physically taxing nature of the work on board ship, he was constantly plagued by seasickness and a feeling that he had not sufficiently recovered from his injuries. However, he held on, hoping to reach Southampton before he collapsed physically. (I suppose my mother's comment on "yoot" with its propensity for resilience would have been appropriate in these circumstances).

After Steven's arrival in Southampton, he and other immigrants were met by the agent of the West Indian Commission, which had been established to help enlighten Caribbean immigrants about English culture. In the weeks after the agent had temporarily housed him in a dormitory, Steven's search for work became desperate as the remainder of his money dwindled. He made friends with other West Indians in London, becoming familiar with others similarly unemployed and desperate, others who in their hunger sometimes lured, caught and cooked pigeons to survive. There was no hope of money from home since his parents did not have it. Finally, he found a variety of menial, low-paying jobs—dishwasher, janitor, park grounds cleaner.

He bought books with what little money he had left from his wages and began to study for the GCE "Advanced" Level, the exam he would have taken if he had remained in high school at home and which would have made him eligible for the Guiana Scholarship and entry to an English university. (There was no university in British Guiana at that time). When he could not buy a particular book, he would read it in bookstores and make hurried, furtive notes until some hyper-vigilant store clerk asked him to buy the book or leave. (The nearest library was too far off, and he could not afford the cost of transportation). He was certain that if he taught himself and studied hard enough, he could pass the exam and perhaps be eligible for a grant to an English university. At this time in London, many penniless students, young women and men from Africa, Asia, the Caribbean and other parts of the British Commonwealth, were in circumstances similar to his. They formed a network, lending each other books and helping each other over the humps of academic achievement. In June 1964, wearing the same pair of pants (now worn and grease-stained) with which he had boarded the *Willemstadt* on the night of *Diwali*, his hands roughened by constant immersion in hot dishwater at the Lambeth teashop where he worked, his nerves frayed by hunger and anxiety, he took the "Advanced" Level exam in five subjects. He passed all five, with distinctions in four. As a British subject, he was now eligible for a British government grant to enter one of the English universities. He was admitted to London University in 1964 and graduated four years later with first-class honors. As was the case when he was the eleven-year old "lad who had topped the colony," all that he had needed was a chance to prove himself.

Amid the chatter and music of the 'Kaiteur,' I reminded him of the day of the scholarship exam when Miss Oz had wrapped him, sick with fever, in a blanket and taken him on Leon's bus to sit for the scholarship exam. At the mention of Miss Oz, he became sadly reflective. She had died ten years after he left home, before he could ever see her again. He stared pensively at the picture of Guyana's Kaiteur Falls on the restaurant wall.

"She kept writing me to come home for a visit, and I kept promising that I would, but something always came up. Subconsciously, I believe I've always resented her for her attitude toward Drew. Sometimes I feel she was just as big a racist as Balgobin, and then I'm torn with guilt because I know she also played a large part in bringing me to what I am today."

His mood changed and he laughed.

"You know Ma was never one to spare the rod! When push came to shove, she would never restrict herself to what were considered to be approved disciplinary instruments like the belt. She would resort to pelting shoes or whatever came to hand." He smiled ruefully.

"I suppose if she used those methods here today, she would be accused of child abuse."

"I think my marrying Julia finally took the wind out of her sails," he murmured.

"Who's Julia?"

"She's a white woman I met and married the year after I went up to London. Ma just couldn't get over it. Pity she never lived long enough to meet my second wife who was Black and Trinidadian." He said this with a faint touch of bitter derision.

"I guess by the time you first married, you had gotten Drew out of your system."

"You know," he said quietly, "I never really did."

Then he added, "In '74, I went home for Ma's funeral. Stayed three days. The day after the funeral, I went up to the Courentyne to see if I could locate Drew. People in the area told me she, Ramdat and their children had emigrated to Toronto some years before. Apparently, when Ramdat got drunk enough, he would beat the daylights out of her, but it seems like she hung on."

His deep sigh appeared to come from some inner bottomless cavern.

"Sometimes it all seems so distant and almost inconsequential—unreal, now," he said. "Almost as though it had happened to someone else."

Fingering his nearly empty glass, he asked me if I wanted another drink. I said no and got up to leave. He signalled the waitress for another rum and coke ("ten-year old *X-M* if you please, the best among the aristocrats of all rums"). I could not help eerily thinking how like Mr. Osbourne he looked as he raised his glass. I had learned from him that Mr. Osbourne had been confined to his home with a stroke soon after Miss Oz's death.

It was near eleven when I rose to leave. Steven stood up, gave me a last hug, and we promised to keep in touch. There was little in the sophisticated, mature man who now stood before me that suggested anything of the once poor, sickly scholarship boy—little, that is, except the fleeting sadness and regret in his eyes, and the ever so faint slump of his shoulders. As I walked out into the cold semi-darkness of Georgia Avenue, Steven put the glass to his lips and drained it. Someone inside the 'Kaieteur' had put on Eddie Hooper's "Passing Memories."

CHAPTER 24

Apart from Shirley's death and the racial violence of the sixties, the other traumatic event in my coming of age in British Guiana was my father's decision not to return to us. With a sigh and the matter-of-fact finality of someone who has read aloud the last lines of a book that she would soon close, my mother announced to Bernard and me one day that my father would not be coming home again. It appeared that he had met another woman in the interior and started another family. Thirty-four years later, I still rummage through the clutter of memory in search of the reasons for his decision and marvel at the ease with which he could walk away from those who loved him and whom he loved. In spite of all the differences I had with my mother, this was something I was certain she would never—*could* never do.

I recalled that over the past weeks, my mother had seemed quieter than usual. Sometimes at night, I would sit bolt upright thinking that I had heard her crying in her bedroom, but then I would go back to sleep with the uneasy feeling that either she or I had been dreaming or that I had not really heard her. I had been so distracted by Drupattie and Steven's departure that I had barely noticed the quietness that had slowly and recently begun creeping over her like the ivy on our bannister rails. Over the years, my father's letters to us and his visits home from the interior had grown increasingly infrequent. It seemed that the cavernous mouth of the great Mazaruni had slowly swallowed him and that he was no longer a part of us. But my mother held us together. She put aside her grief and, more than ever, became like the large old spice mango tree in our front yard—strong and protective.

I find it difficult to relate this part of our experiences because I am torn by conflicting emotions—bitterness and anger at my father and genuine love and admiration for him. Bitterness and anger because his leaving without a proper goodbye increased the emotional distance between him and me and because it left a gaping, bleeding hole in all our souls—even his. Admiration because he never flinched to confront (often successfully) the inequities of the colonial system as they affected him personally, and in so doing, he ultimately provided his children with a fine example of dignity and courage in struggle's ring. Admiration because he saved many lives in the largely underdeveloped, remote, mountainous Mazaruni forest. A slightly eccentric, often solitary man, he read Shakespeare's sonnets in the rivers' stillness, sometimes performed surgery by lamplight, treated yaws, tuberculosis and other daunting illnesses, and eased new life into the world in adverse medical conditions. Today, a living testament to life's bewildering complexity, he is an old man who has been able to come to terms with his human weaknesses, and from the easy chair on his verandah, he stares confidently into the accusing, yet finally forgiving, face of old age.

In his early teens, Bernard often talked of joining the priesthood, inspired by Jesuit-father-teachers at the Catholic High School for boys that he attended in Brickdam. It was the same school that Father Manuel Gomes, (he of earlier physical tribulations in Mr. Davis scholarship class), had later attended. In some way, I think that such thoughts which guaranteed a heavenly sire, eased the longings of Bernard's soul for his absent earthly father.

'Gatha had resumed her sewing in earnest and was now making dresses for the wives of Canadian diplomats. Some of her friends remarked to her, "Gyurl, yuh *shittin' in high grass,* to be shore!" After Eustace's death, she had gone to Superintendent Nelson Irving and told him that she was Eustace's child-mother and that she felt she and her children were entitled to some portion of Eustace's "widows and orphans" benefits. However, Irving informed her that there was no provision in Civil Service regulations for surviving former common-law wives and (what the colonial government glibly and condescendingly regarded in their regulations as) "the illegitimate issue of police officers." Besides, as Irving sniffed through his burnished orange moustache, Eustace had not been killed in the line of duty. Therefore, the police administration had no obligation to provide for his survivors. Indeed, in the eyes of Irving and his fellow senior officers, Eustace's actions had put him outside the fraternal pale of the police and among the criminal elements whom they so scorned.

Among Eustace's peers, however, he was seen as a poor victim of a woman who was rotten to the core. Of course, awed as 'Gatha was by the overwhelming aura of power that Irving exuded by way of his starched, brightly buttoned khaki uniform and the photographs on his office wall of Queen Elizabeth, the Duke of Edinburgh, former English governors, Colonial Secretaries and Chiefs of Police, it never occurred to her to ask for a copy of those regulations. She merely looked crestfallen, wiped her sweating brow, played with her cracked fingernails and embroidered handkerchief, said almost inaudibly, "T'ank yuh very much, suh," rose and prepared to walk back to the Stabroek bus terminus.

As 'Gatha was about to leave his office, Nelson Irving must have heard something to which, of all colonial expatriates, he was the most sensitive: He must have caught in her tone (even with the brevity of her response), the disquieting chord of human yearning for solace that echoes through so much of life's symphony yet is audible only to those who would both hear *and* listen. The hopeless stoop of her shoulders, the seeming vulnerability in her large, soft plaits must have propelled his thoughts back to his own mother now mouldering in a Liverpool cemetery, his mother, a widow who had struggled courageously to raise six children in wartime London and who had finally fallen before the powerful twin adversaries of poverty and mental illness.

"Sit down," he said, perhaps trying to hide the gentleness that threatened to creep into his tone.

Obediently, she sat down again, conscious of the overhead fan creaking rhythmically and cutting laboriously through the thick heat.

"How are you supporting yourself?" he inquired, no doubt striving to make his tone as official, impersonal and disinterested as possible.

Irving was known to take pride in his reputation, and he must have strained to assure himself that 'Gatha did not misunderstand the motives behind his inquiry. Balgobin's sister-in-law, Kamla, was a maid at the Georgetown Club, where she once overheard a warning remark that Irving made to a colonial recruit as both men sipped gin and tonic. Irving told him that local working class women tended to regard as suggestive of ulterior designs, too many personal (even though innocent and kindly) inquiries from men in their positions.

Therefore, as he now dealt with 'Gatha, Irving struggled to maintain aloofness even as he was driven by a genuine interest in her welfare. He probably had enough clout to override the colonial administrative arrangements that slammed the door on her access to benefits. Yet, he did not use such influence because he might not have wanted 'Gatha to mistake his aim (something in her demeanor might have suggested that she would) and because his own professional colleagues might also have wondered about his purpose. No doubt, he found it difficult to decide which was more distasteful: having those of his own social position conjecture about his good intentions (which, as everyone knew, paved the road to hell) or those of 'Gatha's class question his integrity.

"Suh, A does sew, suh" she replied. "But is not always enough, suh," she added timidly.

"I know wives of Canadian diplomats who are looking for a good sempstress. Would you be interested in the work?"

"Yuh mean a seamstress, suh? A dressmaker? A *worker*?"

'Gatha was confused by his pronunciation, and she had to make sure of what he meant.

"Yes. Yes," he answered impatiently, tapping his fingers on his desk. He had heard his friends' wives talking about their difficulty in finding a good seamstress and in getting suitable clothes from abroad for the colony's hot weather.

"Yes suh. I would be in-*tres*-ted," she replied instantly. "Very in-*tres*-ted. Is how many ladies?"

"Well initially, I can think of at least three, but there could be others, and I am willing to make sure that you get a good price for your trouble."

'Gatha was momentarily disconcerted. Shore she wanted to sew fuh di' ladies. Shore she wanted di' lil wuk. But she alone could'n do it. She would have to find two helpers.

He assured her that he would see what he could do, and she rose to leave.

She would see if she could put enough promise into her smile so that Leon would give her a free ride back to Kitty since she did not have enough money for the return trip.

She had told my mother that the last time she had gotten on his bus, they had both exchanged meaningful glances and some low-toned remarks, during which he asked how she and her children were "gettin' along since de det" and whether they all liked Buxton Spice mangoes. An' of course, who in deh right mine doan like Buxton Spice? He had then quickly run into Stabroek Market and bought three extra-large Buxton spice mangoes, which he presented to her when he returned to the bus. Of course his passengers had sat there and fumed, but Leon, as always, was staunchly impervious to their impatience.

"Look! *I got brekfus fuh guh guh cook!*" one woman shrieked as she saw him get up and run off the bus.

"Time doan mean a *dam'* t'ing to dis *blasted* man," said another frustrated female Kittician who was accustomed to Leon's treating the bus as though it were his private home. "Is time somebody report 'e to de Transport and Harbours Department."

Of course, no one ever did.

The daunting specter of Eustace as a romantic rival had disappeared from Leon's field of vision, and he was determined to take advantage of this circumstance. After Leon left the bus, his passengers had resorted to *t'rowin' remarks*, "cutting" their eyes in 'Gatha's direction, steupsing their teeth, and talking of men who ran after "ev'ry *skyut* tail in sight" and women nowadays who "yuh only had to squeeze deh head an' deh legs would open."

'Gatha had settled herself comfortably into a corner seat at the back and ignored them, focussing her attention on the assortment of dray carts, handcarts, trucks, jeeps, lorries, vans, buses, private cars, hire cars, Booker's taxis, cyclists, shoppers, civil servants on their lunch break, beggars, various yelling street vendors of lottery tickets ("if yuh haven' got a ticket, yuh haven' got a chance"), *New Testaments*, bottles, mangoes, coconut water, coconut jelly, cassava pone, coconut buns, sugar cake, mitai, genips, popsicles, shave ice, ice blocks, fudge, *bara*, sweet drinks, mauby, ginger beer, wild canes, pointer brooms, straw mats, dress and pants "material," fried fish, fresh fish, live chickens, exercise books, tripe, pencils, *Lighthouse* cigarettes, *stinkin' toe, commandin' oil, confusion powder, asafetida, cappadula, cocksion, Dodd's Kidney Pills, Sloan's Liniment, DeWitt's Pills, Zex Soap, O.K Soap, Thermogene Medicated Rub, Vicks Cough Drops, Limacol* ("the freshness of a breeze in a bottle"), brilliantine, *Bush Rum, Nugget Shoe Polish, Whizz* and *Phensic* headache tablets, *Edger Boy* and *Breakaday* biscuits, matches, and cook-up rice—all comprising the noisy, colorful, pulsating, wonderful life of Stabroek Market Square.

Leon returned, bounding up the bus steps, and presented her with the Buxton spice mangoes, saying "Heh gyurl, *kerry dis guh gi' dem chirrun.* Afta rall, if A like de cow, I en mus' like de kyaf?"

He laughed heartily, tilting his head back, made a single clap with his hands, vigorously rubbed them together, looked smilingly down and around at the other passengers and said cheerfully, "All aboard fuh Kitty!" as he made his way past the glaring passengers down the narrow aisle to the driver's seat. Miss Ada always said that "Leon only had to sniff a woman an' was like 'e guh crazy." 'Gatha had bestowed on him what she imagined was her most shyly seductive smile, silently damned her decaying front tooth, thanked him for all to hear, and tucked the sweet-smelling, mouth-watering Buxton spice mangoes into her straw bag. The bus screeched protestingly out of Stabroek to the sound of an irritated chorus of sucked teeth.

Two weeks later, with donations from Leon, my mother and Miss Oz and with generous cash advances from two prospective Canadian customers promised by Irving, 'Gatha went down to Auto Supplies Dealers at Hadfield and High

Streets and paid down on a brand new *Necchi* electric sewing machine. Gwennie Braithwaite, whose mother had taught her and 'Gatha to sew, left her domestic employers and joined 'Gatha in what the two of them jokingly referred to as "de sempstress business." Some months later, they hired two assistants—apprentices—"sewing gyurls"—to help with basting, hemming, other "hand work," pressing and sweeping up bits of material, while 'Gatha and Gwennie undertook the more important business of taking measurements, cutting out and machine stitching.

Before long, they were receiving so many orders from their Canadian clients that my mother was losing patience because of the time 'Gatha took to getting around to sew my school uniforms. Besides, 'Gatha never seemed to have time nowadays for the usual chit-chat, something I think my mother sorely missed at this time. Nelson Irving made good on his promise: 'Gatha and Gwennie were so busy that they rented larger quarters, and in the interests of efficiency, Gwennie moved in with 'Gatha.

By October 1963, Leon had also moved in.

Leon and 'Gatha had been talking of getting married, and so Gwennie decided that she had to leave. But while both women were doing better financially, the prohibitive expense of housing made it difficult for Gwennie to find affordable accommodation. One of their Canadian clients, Gwennie's former employer, suggested that she apply for the Canadian domestic program in which, every year, through a process of elimination, thirty women were selected for domestic work in Canada. It was a way out, a way for women with few prospects to break out of the circle of poverty. Gwennie's former employer was willing to provide her with outstanding references and to act as a sponsor, both matters that tipped the outcome in her favor. 'Gatha's reputation and clientele were now firmly established, and she should have no difficulty securing a replacement for Gwennie, who also realized that going to Canada would put her in a better position to take care of her ailing mother. Besides, Gwennie would have gone anywhere to escape the tired, tiring drone of sewing machines, and after her domestic servitude in Montreal was over, to explore, if possible, what life was like in the rest of the world.

On the center pages of the *Daily Chronicle* in mid-November 1963, a picture appeared of thirty young women—two East Indian women who stand together off to the side a little self-consciously and twenty-eight black women ranging in dusky shades from what was then considered to be sappodilla brown, through what might be coffee or mahogany, depending on the quality of the black-and-white photograph. Most of these women of color already look "foreign," standing on the tarmac at Atkinson Field in two-piece suits with heavy coats draped over their stiffly crooked arms. Some of them appear glum; others smile at the *Chronicle* cameraman, Viv MacDonald, in a stiff, hopeful, pose. On one side of the group is Miss Matheson, the Civil Servant who represents the Labour Department, and on the other is the Canadian representative in the British Consulate. The British West Indian Airways propeller plane, which will take them first to Trinidad, waits like some expectant, giant, metallic, pale yellow bird.

The photograph's caption reads "Thirty domestics pose for cameraman Viv MacDonald at Atkinson Field yesterday, minutes before leaving colony for Trinidad *en route* to Canada." I recognize Gwennie standing squarely in the middle of the group, a little Jackie Kennedy type of white pillbox hat on her head, a pair of beigeish-looking gloves on her hands. She looks like one of the young women in *Ebony* or *Tan* magazine, women we looked at and imagined becoming when we were little girls.

Leon had driven Gwennie to the airport in his taxi, and 'Gatha and I had also gone along to see her off. We were her family in the last days before she left. Her mother was too sick to go to the airport, her father was off drunk somewhere, and her brothers could not be bothered. After Drupattie's departure, Gwennie and I had grown closer. 'Gatha had bought the material and sewn her outfit as a farewell gift. Miss Ida had brought a little fruitcake for her to "sweeten she mout' wid" and ease her homesickness as she got accustomed to Canada. Because Gwennie's own mother had never been able to give her bangles, my mother and I agreed to have a single gold bangle made for her from my two baby bracelets. Gwennie's new bangle was pure British Guiana gold. Miss Oz had given her a tightly wrapped package of guava cheese. Leon, failing to consider the possible vigilance of the Canadian authorities, had tucked two Buxton Spice mangoes into her luggage. Thus it was that Gwennie arrived at Atkinson Field without her "true-true" family, yet warmly wrapped in the love of the community against the prospect of the Canadian cold.

Today when I look at the yellowed clipping of the *Chronicle* photograph, I cannot help thinking that the young woman standing in the center of the group—the pretty, coffee-colored young woman—had the truest, sweetest smile of them all.

CHAPTER 25

In my heart I was sure that December 1963 would be my last Christmas in British Guiana. True, I was attracted to Michael Dover, but there seemed to be little left in the colony for me then. I had a clear sense that my life was in transition, that I had come to an inevitable fork in the road. Belinda was making plans to join her parents in London, and she would be gone by the end of the Christmas term. (Many people seemed to be looking for a means of escape from the racial troubles). Michael showed little inclination to explore the world. The horizon of his ambition seemed limited to the local Civil Service after high school, with cricket, rugby, and dominoes in the after-hours to break the monotony. I had done creditably well on the GCE exam and had applied to Howard University in Washington D.C., where I was accepted for the next year as an English major. I really had no idea how I would manage financially after my first semester in Washington, but I was determined to go. My mother, usually so protective, kept urging me to go, to leap out into the dark, trusting in what she considered to be the efficacious combination of God's strength and my "yoot" to see me through. My parents had been able to save only a small sum, but my mother made me believe that somehow we would find a way. Had it not been for her nudging, the absolute steadfastness of her faith that I would succeed, her undivided, unswerving dedication to her children's having a better life than she, I might never have taken the plunge. But I did.

"Dere is nutting like a profession for a woman," she would say to me. "Men come an' go, but you will always have yuh papers an' dat is de one t'ing nobody will ever be able to take from you. Nobody!"

She would say this with startling vehemence. In the wake of my GCE results, it seemed that I would yet elude the (to her) daunting specter of becoming a shop girl at Booker's. But Michael caused her even greater concern. The last thing she wanted was for me to "bring in a belly" as she so descriptively put it. So after I had been increasingly late getting home from meetings with Michael, she became irate.

"You Miss Lady," she started, working herself up to a slow sizzle. "You know what you playin' wid? You see any decent young gyurl out at dis time?"

Of course, Miss Ida might have been keeping her informed of my movements, and for my part, I felt that my mother was treating me annoyingly like a child. After all, I was seventeen years old, for God's sake!

"Why do you keep t'inkin' dat what happened to you will happen to me? Give me some credit for good sense!" I yelled at her.

This seemed to take her completely by surprise because she was not accustomed to such opposition, and worse, I appeared to have touched some raw, painful nerve. Two seconds of thick, pregnant silence elapsed before she suddenly and forcefully struck out at me with Bernard's belt that appeared as if from nowhere.

"Yuh playin' a big woman?" she asked, striking again. "Two big women kyant live in de same house!"

These words were punctuated by the motion of the belt and its "wapping" sound-sting on my flesh. Somewhere from the recesses of the past, my childhood humiliation in Mr. Davis' scholarship class came rushing back. Silent rage born of powerlessness merged with the frustration of incomplete closure—my father's leaving, and Shirley's leaving, and Drupattie's leaving and Steven's leaving, and, soon, my own leaving. I resolved that I would never—never again tolerate anyone striking me without trying to protect myself. I grabbed the belt; we had a brief tussle for it, and I was finally able to tear it forcefully from her grasp. It seemed that "yoot" was indeed on my side.

Fatigue appeared to overwhelm her; she stared at me for a long time, those large eyes filling with tears, and then turned and went into her bedroom.

How strange, I thought, that she would entrust me to the dark unknown, the leap out across the ocean, but not to the arms of a man—even one whom she knew.

Ole people seh, *"Eye na see, heart na bun."*

I woke that morning with a faintly perceptible buzzing in my head, my eyes searching the grey gloom for the first streaks of sunlight which would signal the day. Far away in the distance, a cock crowed, and a dog's savage bark was followed by a metallic clanging and rhythmic scraping. I knew it was Balgobin, the milkman, approaching the front of our house. I knew too that soon I would hear his loud curses as he tried desperately to shake Rufus the Rice-Eater from his trouser leg. I lay in bed knowing I was visualizing the scene quite accurately: The milkman would be performing a frantic balancing act on the rusty old *Raleigh* bike, trying to keep from falling and spilling the precious cow's milk from the enormous metal containers hanging from his handlebars by wire-like handles. He would kick out at the mangy old dog, turning the handlebars sharply from side to side and causing the bike to swerve from one side of the deserted road to the other, waking the sleeping street with the loud clatter of metal. In his frustration, the milkman added loud curses to his efforts, and his cries seemed to give voice to the silent protesting fears of Kitty's slumbering poor. But the aging Rufus was dogged. He would keep his fangs hooked into Balgobin's tattered trouser hem until he developed enough speed and balance to outstrip him. By this time Rufus would be joined by his unruly dog pals, all barking to signal their complicity, but also showing their fear of the force of the old discarded policeman's boot that Balgobin wore.

It was 1964 and I had just become eighteen. I awoke to the realization that the next day I would be leaving British Guiana for a long time. I would go first to New York and then on to Washington, D.C., where I would live in the University's Crandall Hall until I found work. There would be no money for vacation visits. Leon would take my family down to Atkinson Field, and we would stop at my grandmother's on the way to the airport. My father had come from the interior to say goodbye. The elation that I felt at the prospect of being on my own was suddenly replaced by panic at what I was about to embark on. A cold fear gripped me. Suppose the whole venture did not work out. What would I do in a strange city—country—where I knew scarcely anyone? I started to feel like a condemned prisoner on the day before an execution until I remembered my mother's firm words of encouragement and the way she always faced struggle head-on. I also recalled that she never tired of recounting the Joe Louis-Max Schmelling return bout, in which the courageous Joe Louis, the dogs of racism yapping around his heels, knocked Schmelling out so fast that people who had gathered in eager anticipation around village cake shop radios hardly had time to take the first sip of their *gamby*.

The sound of a man's screaming mingled with that of dogs' barking and running footsteps on Lamaha Street. I peered out as lights went on in some houses along the street.

Balgobin lay on the street, blood streaming from his body. I barely glimpsed the figures of Joe-Joe, Fine T'ings, Winston and Bruk-up running madly away from the crime scene around the corner into Pike Street. Balgobin lay where they left him, blood streaming from his prone form. He started to groan. Mr. Jacobs, who had risen early to go over his shop books, and Miss Oz, who was getting ready to feed her hens, saw and heard him when they came out of their gates and into the street. To no one in particular, Mr. Jacobs yelled, "Ketch dem! Ketch dem!" as he pointed in the direction of the fleeing young men. Gradually, people, awakened by the commotion, emerged into the street, mingling with the barking dogs around Balgobin. Someone vigorously kicked Rufus the Rice-eater, who had inched closer, along with other barking dogs attracted by the smell of blood. He yelped in an almost human voice, then went off whining-whimpering down the street, his tail between his legs. *He paused, watching, waiting for a chance to return to the scene.* Bahadur, the market grocer, came out and slowly and sadly stooped and cradled Balgobin's head. Balgobin had been stabbed in the right chest and abdomen. Daddy Pads yelled, "Alyou get a taxi quick-quick!" Miss Oz returned to her house and brought back some "sweet sugar water" (a palliative in instances like these) for Balgobin to drink. Soon several hands were lifting him into the back of a cream-colored *Austin Devon* hire car that sped off for the Public Hospital. Some in the group were heard to mutter that Balgobin "had it comin', an' it good fuh 'e. Afta rall, *do suh na like suh.*" (Later my mother wrote telling me that Balgobin had recovered from his wounds).

Banga Mary, the derelict madwoman who lived under the awning of Mr. Jacob's shop, hovered on the fringes of the growing crowd. As children, when we grew tired of teasing her, we would conduct conversations with her, and if we heard *and* listened to what she was saying, sometimes we discovered that she made sense. Many of the adults had no time to waste on Banga Mary, her jaws continually moving around toothless gums, her rags flapping about her. She was now saying to no one in particular that she had overheard Joe-Joe and his confederates planning to take violent revenge on Balgobin for what he had done to Steven. If this was so, then their plans fit neatly into the prevailing climate of racial unrest.

"Race hate... race hate... race hate," Banga Mary murmured as though she were soothing an infant. "One day race hate will mek dis country choke in it own blood," she cackled crazily.

Those who heard her were either unwilling to consider her mutterings or uncaring about their implication—or both.

Afta rall, de woman was as mad as a hatter.

I went back into the house to finish packing.

Glossary of Guyanese Colloquialisms

2. *Catcher:* a simple child's game in which one child runs after the other to "tag" or "catch" him so that the other becomes "it." The two roles are then switched.

   Coloured Girl in the Ring: a "ring play" game that usually involves little girls. However, it is also played by women during queh-queh festivities, and boys may also participate. The players form a circle in which they join hands and sing the folksong "Coloured Girl in the Ring." A female player in the center performs the instructions of the lyrics as they are sung by those who form the circle.

   Author's note: I have used the British spelling for "coloured" and other such words so as to ground the work firmly in its English colonial setting.

5. *Kunumunu:* stupid person

8. *Senseh:* breed of scraggly-feathered fowl

12. *Obeah:* of West African origin, body of local supernatural beliefs and practices

    Spit Press: rumour mill

13. *Rass:* (expletive)

    Nugget: brand of shoe polish

    Lighthouse: brand of cheap local cigarettes

14. *Souse:* boiled pieces of cow's face, pig's feet, and/or 'cow heel' pickled with vinegar and seasonings

    To: too

    Cuttas: small appetizers used to complement alcoholic beverages

15. *Pulourie*: East Indian delicacy that is a thick batter of ground split peas, flour, curry, cumin, salt and pepper, fried as small balls
    Channa: chickpeas
    Pine tarts: small pineapple pies
16. *Child-father*: unmarried father of a child
17. *De visitors from Red China*: the menstrual period
    Gangasaka: green lizard
18. *Madam*: owner of a home-based hairdressing business who would sometimes employ a number of young female apprentices
    Winin': dancing with seductive hip movements
    Trench: narrow drainage canal running along some road sides
19. *Runner*: cow's intestine
20. *Woman alone is like tin cup; ev'rybody wan' pass an'dip dey han'*: (Creole saying) A woman on her own is considered easy prey for those who wish to use her.
    An' to besize: and, too, besides
    Before de spirit ketch yuh: before you were filled with religious zeal
    If yuh mek yuhself grass, goat gun eat yuh: (Creole saying) If you leave yourself vulnerable, then you will become a victim.
21. *Does tek food pun tick*: take food on credit
    Using a tick or check mark, some local shopkeepers and other vendors would note their customers' purchases on scraps of paper that they hooked on wall nails. At the end of a particular period, the shopkeeper would bill the customer. This system required *trust* on both sides of the counter. Indeed, the word, "trust,"or colloquially, *truss*, is also used as a synonym for the phrase, *tek pun tick*.
23. *Is not de fuss pickney I mine*: This will not be the first child I have cared for.
    Goods: groceries
24. *Littie*: played mostly by girls, a game like 'jacks' that uses, instead, small stones

Fufu: Of Nigerian and other West African origin, this is a very thick paste made from boiled green plantains that one pounds in a mortar using a long wooden pestle.

Breakfast: heavy midday meal comparable in its nutritive content to dinner in the metropole

27. *Sugar cake:* confection made with coconut, spice and sugar

Genips: small, usually sweet, one-seeded fruit with smooth green disposable skin

31. *Breathing short:* hyperventilating

35. *Puttah puttah:* thick, liquid mud

36. *Rumsucker, VanDrunkenburg:* terms of abuse directed at an alcoholic

39. *Nineted:* anointed

Sapping: patting (a liquid) on the skin with a cloth

45. *Brickdam:* simply referred to as "Brickdam," one of the oldest streets in Georgetown, dating back to times when the city was essentially a small colonial trading outpost

49. *Apaan Jhat:* each race for itself

50. *Kyat eat alyou dinner:* You will lose everything.

Child-mother: the unmarried mother of a child. The primary significance of the terms, child-mother and *child-father* (page 16), resides not in the relationship of each to the child, but in that of each to the other, as in wife and husband.

53. *Ricketts Crown:* the brand name of cakes of blue used in the whitening of clothes during laundering

Steam: resort to obeah in food preparation in order to secure a lover's affection

Goat en bite me: I am presentable. There is nothing wrong with me.

Kineness mek crappo en got tail: (Creole saying) The frog's overly generous nature led to the loss of its tail.

54. *Talkin' name:* gossiping

55. *School-leaving:* examination that certified that a pupil had satisfactorily completed the elementary 'standards' or grades

60. *Pupil-teacher:* Requiring the prerequisite of a school-leaving certificate, the pupil-teacher examination was taken in elementary school by students who showed the character, aptitude and inclination for a teaching career at the elementary level. This examination was taken in stages, and often the village headmaster would teach extra lessons to 'pupil-teacher students' just as he would to the scholarship students. 'Pupil-teacher' students were afforded practice in teaching lower grades or 'standards,' but they were often subject to the same disciplinary measures meted out to regular students.

66. *Demerara:* pertaining to the county of Demerara

68. *Tek she belly an' mek it buryin' grung:* have an abortion
    Kyan: can't

69. *Dung tung:* downtown

71. *She is de kyat's mudduh; he is de four-footed fadduh:* usually said aggressively, a retort that has less meaning than venom
    Whuh yuh en put dung: what does not belong to you
    Crosses: distress

72. *Labaria:* poisonous local snake

75. *Queh-queh:* considered to be of West African tradition, pre-wedding festivities that are centered on the bride

77. *Don' put yuh mout' in big people business:* Stay out of older people's affairs.
    Fas': inquisitive

79. *Address the house properly:* show respect to the household

80. *Typee:* infatuation to the point of being helplessly besotted

81. *Any cow an' bull foot:* anyone
    Posy: chamber pot
    Shame suh till: very ashamed

82. *Wash deh mout' pun:* gossip maliciously about

85. *Mudflat:* The muddy nature of the coastal terrain, especially in the rainy seasons, led some Guianese to refer to the country by this affectionate nickname.

88. *Logie:* sugar estate shack with roof made of plaited palm leaves

89. *Sun-hot:* intense heat

91. *Yuh cork duck:* You will lose out.
    Boxin' from pillar to pos': lacking direction or purpose
    Mekkin' styles pun 'e: pretending indifference to him
    Voomps pun she: regard her with interest
    T'ief: steal
92. *Clammacherry:* berry with sticky glue-like juice
93. *Coolie t'ing:* racist, sexist reference to an East Indian woman
97. *Pork-knocker:* Timber workers and gold and diamond miners who went into the country's remote, mountainous, forested interior sometimes carried along dried salted pork among their rations. These men came to be known as pork-knockers.
98. *Yard:* A common open area in the center of a group of 'range-type' dwellings, the yard is a common physical and social feature of Caribbean working class life.
99. *Bambye:* leftovers; later
106. *Loose:* let go of
109. *Yoot:* youth
110. *Batchie:* alone—as single persons
111. *House:* seating area of the cinema on the floor between those of the pit and balcony
113. *Ole time story:* stories about their youth
    Coague: milky concoction similar to egg-nog; sometimes also called *flip*
    Rice pap: rice porridge
118. *Bridge:* Trenches that ran in front of dwellings and other buildings were crossed by small, usually wooden, bridges.
119. *Pickney, you a come; you a come:* (Creole saying) Child, in time, you will experience, and so understand, this situation. Drawn from the short creole folk tale: *Pig ask 'e mumma, 'Mumma a wha' mek yuh mout' suh lang?' 'E mumma answer, 'Pickney, you a come; you a come.'*
122. *Camoudi:* non-venomous species of anaconda usually about fifteen to eighteen feet long
123. *She eye pass de man:* She disrespected him.
    Gi'in' 'e blow: being unfaithful to him

124. *Marabunta:* wasp
125. *Gyaff:* converse
127. *Hornin':* being unfaithful; akin to *gi'in blow* (page 123)
129. *Steupsed:* sucked
130. *Time longer dan twine:* (Creole saying) Inevitably, one will have to pay for one's misdeeds.
134. *Bourn-Vita:* brand of chocolate beverage
     Buryin' grung: burying ground; cemetery
     Jumbie: ghost
135. *Sakkiwinky:* small, local wild monkey known for its agility
138. *Pointer:* rib of coconut palm branch
139. *Public Buildings:* legislative meeting rooms
140. *Bata yachtings:* brand of cheap, rubber-soled, laced, canvas shoes
     Jargetung: Georgetown
141. *LCP:* League of Coloured Peoples
148. *Dougla:* the offspring of an East Indian and Black couple
149. *Clappin' roti:* Roti is a local East Indian food made of flattened dough that is cooked on a hot, flat, greased, iron pan called a *tawa*. Immediately after removing it from the *tawa*, one briefly "claps" the cooked dough between one's palms so that it remains soft, flat and flexible.
153. *Pepperpot:* a kind of stew made with spices, seasoned meats and a dark-coloured cassava root derivative called *cassareep*
155. *Porely an' sof'ly:* so-so
156. *Tutorial:* Tutorial High School
     Kyan: can
     Idocity: audacity
157. *Progue:* prod, probe
     Sof'ly, sof'ly, ketch monkey: (Creole saying) Similar to *time longer dan twine* (page 130)
159. *Bruk:* break
160. *Dholl:* thick, liquid East Indian dish consisting of split peas flavoured with curry powder, garlic, onions, and cumin
     Bajie: spinach, also known locally as *calaloo*; Indo-Guyanese also refer to any green leafy vegetable as *bajie*.

162. *Poe great but han' to mout':* proud but poor
164. *Kyan:* can
    Gyap: gap; area of roadway immediately in front of the entrance to one's dwelling
166. *Boat go a falls:* that which seems inevitable occurs
168. *T'ick:* thick, physically well-built
169. *Overdo de do:* over-react
178. *Is wheh 'e deh?:* Where is he?
184. *Shittin' in high grass:* associating with those of a higher social class than she
186. *Worker:* Locally used term for dressmaker
187. *I got brekfus fuh guh guh cook:* I have to go and cook breakfast.
    T'rowin' remarks: making spiteful insinuations
    Skyut: skirt
188. *Bara:* small roti
    Stinkin' toe: smelly, but edible, fruit of the locust tree
    Commandin' oil, confusion powder: substances used in obeah practice
    Asafetida: foul smelling plant resin given to babies for the treatment of worms and sometimes applied to the scalps of some Indo-Guyanese infants to 'ward off evil spirits'
    Cappadula, cocksion: local vines brewed, along with sarsaparilla root and the bark of the locust tree, into a tea that allegedly promotes male sexual potency
    Bush Rum: local bootleg liquor distilled from molasses, sugar, yeast and barley
    Kerry dis guh gi' dem chirrun: Give this to your children.
194. *Eye na see, heart na bun:* (Creole saying) Being unaware of a situation that would otherwise be displeasing renders one immune to feelings of discomfort about it
195. *Gamby:* any alcoholic beverage
196. *Do suh na like suh:* (Creole saying) Those who inflict pain on others dislike being on the receiving end of similar treatment.